Evelyn Wood
READING DYNAMICS®

For Speed, Comprehension, and Retention

Evelyn Wood
READING DYNAMICS®

Eight reasons why this program is one of the best investments you will ever make.

Invest in yourself. Our course brings out the best in you by expanding your tremendous potential. Increase your own personal productivity. You'll use the skills for the rest of your life.

Read faster. You, too, will learn to read two to three times faster than before! Our graduates number more than two million—including U.S. Presidents, cabinet members, legislators, and heads of state.

Understand more. You will experience a dramatic improvement in your reading comprehension. Get a clearer understanding of what you read without having to go over the same material again and again.

Remember more. Our course is designed to maximize retention. Learn to improve your recall—both long- and short-term. Become an informed, effective communicator.

Process information more effectively. You will learn to quickly sift through the vast amount of high-speed information being generated today. Read to make sound decisions far sooner and far more effectively.

Manage your time better. Accomplish more of your goals. Organize your time and your life. Our course will teach you valuable time management skills applicable to every aspect of reading—at work, school, and home.

Reduce your study time. With our course, you will learn more effective study techniques. These skills will help you to excel academically while cutting back on actual study time. Learn valuable note-taking and test-taking strategies.

Enjoy more free time. We saved the best for last! By reading more effectively and managing your time better, you will discover a lot more free time.

Table of Contents

<u>**What You Need for This Lesson:**</u>

Evelyn Wood Course Guide

Audio CD #1

Pencil or pen

> **DO NOT TURN TO THE NEXT**
> **PAGE UNTIL INSTRUCTED TO**
> **DO SO ON THE AUDIO CD.**

Evelyn Wood
READING DYNAMICS®

Lesson 1

Find Your Present Reading Rate

Albert Einstein
by Arthur Beckhard

Chapter One: CHASING THE 'X'

"Why do I have to go to school, Papa?" Hermann Einstein, tall and severe looking, looked down at his ten-year old son. "Do you want to grow up to be an ignoramus, Albert?"   *34*

"What's an ignoramus?"

A burst of laughter came from a corner of the large, comfortably furnished room. Father and son turned quickly toward Mrs. Einstein, who was seated at the large black piano.   *67*

"Oh, Hermann," Mrs. Einstein exclaimed, her voice still bubbling with laughter, "you'll never beat Albert at that game!"

"I'm sure I don't know what you mean," her husband sputtered.   *96*

"There's no use in pretending," Mrs. Einstein replied, as she went on playing an old Hungarian folk song. "I heard you and your brother deciding that the only way to keep Albert from asking so many questions was to answer him by asking him a question. But you see, it didn't work. He can always outlast you!"   *153*

Albert crossed the room and stood beside his mother, for a moment forgetting what he had asked. Her fingers fascinated him. They were such stubby, soft little fingers, and yet they danced and fluttered across the keys with the speed of a robin running across the lawn. They hit the keys so firmly, without fumbling or hesitations, that they made the piano fairly sing. They leaped and pounced upon two final crashing chords. Mrs. Einstein swung herself around on the piano bench and took Albert into her arms.   *241*

She looked over the top of his dark, curly head and smiled up at her husband. "You see, there is a way to make Albert stop asking questions. My music will do it." 274

Mr. Einstein nodded, smiling. Before he had a chance to answer, Albert wriggled around in his mother's arms so that he could turn and face her. 300

"Is it wrong to ask questions?" he asked.

Now it was Mr. Einstein's turn to laugh.

"There he goes again!" He chuckled. "Even your music can't stop him for long."

Mrs. Einstein looked at her husband reprovingly, and she gave Albert a small hug. 344

"There's nothing wrong in asking questions," she said fondly, "as long as you don't do it just to tease or embarrass people or to make them seem foolish." 372

"I don't do it like that," the boy protested. "I do it because there is so much I don't know—so much I want to know. I want to know all about everything right away."

Albert's mother smiled proudly, but his father drew his heavy eyebrows together. He looked puzzled.

"If you really mean that, Albert, how is it that you could ask why you must go to school? School is the place where questions should be answered." 450

"But they're not!" Albert cried out. "They don't even let anybody ask questions, and they'd never think of answering them. I hate school! It's like being in prison. The teachers are like prison guards marching up and down between the rows of desks."

Mr. Einstein and his lovely wife exchanged a look that was full of meaning. What could they say in answer to their son's charges? 517

The Einsteins had moved from the little city of Ulm, in Bavaria, in 1880, a year after Albert was born. Mr. Einstein and his brother Jacob, who had foreseen what would happen to Bavaria, had packed up and brought the whole family to Munich. There the two brothers set up a small chemist's shop. They had been there only a year when Albert's little sister, Maja, was born, and the family moved into a large comfortable house just outside the center of town.

600

It was not long before "the Einstein House," as people called it, became one of the most popular places in the whole city of Munich. Often when permanent residents had guests from out of town they took them to the Einstein house for an evening of conversation and music or poetry reading. These evenings were so much discussed that often visitors to Munich would, upon arrival, ask their hosts if they could possibly arrange for an invitation to the Einstein's.

679

An invitation, however, was scarcely necessary. There was nothing formal about these affairs. Sometimes Mrs. Einstein would play Mozart or Brahms compositions. Sometimes she would sing folk ballads of Germany and Austria. On some evenings, the guests all gathered around the piano and sang old songs they all knew. Both Mr. Einstein and his brother had deep, pleasant voices and could lead their guests in these familiar melodies.

748

Many times neighbors and friends gathered just to talk in the warm, friendly living room with its deep maroon wallpaper lighted by the orange glow from the gaslight chandelier that hung from the white ceiling, and the evening sped by without allowing time for any music at all. Young Albert hated to go to bed on these occasions. He listened, wide-eyed, to the talk of new inventions like the electric light and the telephone. His father and Uncle Jacob were well posted on all the latest scientific developments, particularly those which might affect the sale of equipment and the electrochemical apparatus. Their shop was far ahead of their competitors in all such matters.

863

There were times when Albert's father would decide to read aloud from the works of great German writers such as Goethe, Schiller, and Heinrich Heine. Young Albert could never decide which kind of evening at home he liked best. Certainly there was a great contrast between learning in the friendly atmosphere of his own home and the austere school classrooms where the pupils were punished for failure but never given praise or encouragement for accomplishments.   *939*

Mr. and Mrs. Einstein spent a good deal of thought in the selection of a school for Albert. He had been backward as a small child, slow to learn to talk and read, and very shy. They had selected a Catholic school considered the very best in Munich. They were dismayed when the government took over the operation of all the schools and began installing military rules and regulations.   *1008*

"The true culture of Germany is being submerged by militarism," Mr. Einstein exclaimed sadly.

But neither of Albert's parents had realized the extent to which the Prussian army had taken over the public school system until Albert's very real unhappiness became apparent to them.   *1052*

"They make us memorize the day's lesson," the boy told them. "They don't tell us what it says or what it means, but we must learn every single word. And I can't. Unless I know what a thing means, I just can't remember it. And so they open the drawer and take out the ruler..."   *1109*

His mother hugged him and kissed the palm of his hand, still red from the strokes of the steel ruler. She looked up at her husband appealingly. Mr. Einstein shook his head. "There's nothing we can do," he said. "They will question our loyalty if we complain to the principal." He sat down and beckoned Albert to come closer.   *1158*

"Albert," he said, placing a friendly hand on his son's shoulder, "your mother and I don't like this any more than you do, but we must all face it. You are old enough now to understand what is going on in the world around you. The army is becoming more and more important in Germany and in Austria. It will not be long before the army rules the country. Even now, army officers are buying up big businesses. So far they have bought only the larger stores. But soon they will see that Mr. So-and-So has a nice little candy store on the corner. They will buy the store across the street. Then they will tell everyone that they must stop buying candy from Mr. So-and-So and must, instead, buy from the new store. That is the way it usually works out when the military becomes too important."   *1310*

"The real reason why you must go to school is that there is a law in Germany that no one may get a job unless he has a diploma. You will have to finish six more years of primary school and high school before you can get one; and some day you may have to get a job and help me and Uncle Jacob support your mother and little Maja."   *1388*

Albert looked into his father's face and saw that he was not fooling. The situation was serious.

"I won't complain anymore, Father," he said. "I'll try my best to get along in school."   *1422*

Then he turned and, with his head lowered, eyes staring at the flower pattern in the carpet, he started toward the door. In the doorway he turned. *1449*

"Perhaps I could earn money playing my violin," he said. "Then I wouldn't have to have a diploma."   *1465*

"I'm afraid you would have to practice a long time to learn to play well considering the possibility in all seriousness."   *1486*

"Wouldn't mind practicing if I knew why," Albert explained. "And I don't mind it anymore—"

"Albert," his father interrupted, "I don't think it would be a good idea. It's never a good idea to do something you love doing just for money. It always spoils it."

"What's that? What's that I hear?" A big voice shouted from the little foyer just outside the living room. It was Uncle Jacob.

"Hermann, did I hear you telling the boy that it was wrong to get money for doing a job you enjoy? That's poppycock and you know it!" *1600*

Uncle Jacob was a big man, much taller and heavier than Albert's father; his booming voice always seemed to carry a great deal of authority. Now he turned to Albert and addressed him with all the seriousness of a defense attorney pleading his client's case before a judge and jury. *1649*

"My boy, try to understand what I'm saying. You should always try to do work you love. And if you find yourself in a spot where you have to do work that you dislike, you must find a way of making yourself like it so that you can do it well." Albert looked doubtful. He shook his head. "I hate school," he said stubbornly. *1713*

"Albert!" Mr. Einstein said severely. "I don't want you to use that word. There is enough hate in the world without hating such a thing as schoolwork."

He lapsed into silence as Mrs. Einstein put a quieting hand on his arm. Uncle Jacob crossed over to the fireplace and lifted his long porcelain-bowl pipe off the mantel. *1771*

"I think I can show you what I mean, boy," he said. "What subject do you hate most?"

Albert thought for a moment before answering.

"I can't decide between algebra and geometry. I hate — I mean I dislike them both." *1812*

Uncle Jacob grinned.

"There's no reason to hate or dislike either of them. They're both the laziest kind of mathematics. Look, I want you to try something, an experiment." *1841*

He paused for a moment and Albert waited.

"Do you ever play policemen, or pirates, or anything like that?" Uncle Jacob asked. *1863*

"Sure."

"Well, try playing detective for a change. You're looking for a villain. You don't know whether he's a thief or a pickpocket. You don't even know his name. All you're sure of is that he's somewhere around and you've got to find him to keep him from doing any harm. First thing you do is give him a name for your files. Right?" *1929*

Albert nodded. his eyes glistening with excitement. "You call him 'X'."

Again Albert nodded.

"Then you tail him. You follow him into one formula and out of it and into another or you slide down the hypotenuse of a triangle after him and chase him up the side wall of a parallelogram. Finally you catch up with him. You find out what he is and who he is. Now you've got him! You put the cuffs on him and take him in. That's all algebra is. Or geometry. Like to give it a try?"

"Yes." Albert said earnestly, "I would. I think that would help a lot." *2036*

If you finish early...

If you finish reading *Chasing the "X"* before the tone sounds, IMMEDIATELY BEGIN TIMING the amount of time left until the tone sounds. To compute your reading rate:

- Round off the amount of time you did not use to the nearest quarter minute. For example, 11 seconds would be 1/4 minute.

- Subtract the amount of time you did not use from three minutes to find the amount of time you did use.

- Divide the total number of words (2,036) by the amount of time you used.

Chasing the "X" Quiz

1. Mrs. Einstein was seated: (67 words)
   - a. at an electric organ.
   - b. on a round piano stool.
   - c. at a large black piano.
   - d. at a small well-tuned piano.

2. Mrs. Einstein had the long tapering fingers of an artist. (241 words)
   True (False)

3. Albert's curiosity was: (468 words)
   - a. satisfied by the demands of school.
   - b. unsatisfied because teachers didn't let anyone ask questions.
   - c. limited to science.
   - d. challenged by the game he played with his father.

4. The Einsteins had moved from the city of _____ in Bavaria in 1880. (531 words)

5. Albert's sister was named: (600 words)
   - a. Marie.
   - b. Marta.
   - c. Maja.
   - d. Mara.

6. The Einstein house was: (679 words)
   - a. where Mrs. Einstein played her own compositions.
   - b. so popular that it was necessary to have an invitation to go there.
   - c. a friendly place with its blue living room and its subdued lighting.
   - d. one of the most popular places in the city of Munich.

7. The Einstein brothers sold electro-chemical apparatus in their shop. (863 words)
   True   False

Continued on the next page.

8. Albert, as a small child, had been: (1008 words)
   a. backward, slow to read and learn.
   b. average.
   c. outgoing and friendly.
   d. happy in the friendly atmosphere of school.

9. Albert, as a child, attended a Catholic school in _____.
   (1008 words)

10. The Prussian army: (1052 words)
    a. was criticized by the Einsteins because of their school methods.
    b. had very little effect on the schools.
    c. took over all the schools.
    d. took over the public but not the parochial schools.

Calculating Comprehension Scores

Number of Questions Responsible for Answering

		1	2	3	4	5	6	7	8	9	10
	1	100	50	33	25	20	16	14	13	11	10
	2		100	67	50	40	33	29	25	22	20
	3			100	75	60	50	43	38	33	30
	4				100	80	67	57	50	44	40
	5					100	83	72	63	56	50
	6						100	86	75	67	60
	7							100	88	78	70
	8								100	89	80
	9									100	90
	10										100

Number of Answers Correct

"Jack and Jill" Recall Sheet

Write major points in the column on the left and details or supporting points in the column on the right.

More Important Points	Details & Supporting Points
Jack and Jill climb hill	
	for water
Jack falls	
	breaks "crown"
	Jill tumbles, too

Whether an item is more important or a detail is subjective; there is no right or wrong on this evaluation.

Recall Sheet

Write everything you remember from the selection you have read. Do NOT look back at the reading. Write only one item on each line.

More Important Points	Details & Supporting Points
playing piano	to stop questions
Question game	with Dad
Kept asking question	Boy
not able to ask eshool	Boy
Mom + Dad joking	
Mom had fat fingus	
No one could stop questions	

Go on to the next page if you need more room.

Recall Sheet (continued)

More Important Points	Details & Supporting Points

Total number of Important Points:_____7_____

Total number of Supporting Points: _____4_____

Could you have written more with more time: _____No_____

Average words per minute reading rate: _____150_____

Set Your Reading Goal

The average reader reads at a rate somewhat below 240 words per minute. Now that you have completed the beginning reading evaluation, you can evaluate your own reading skills using the chart below.

Under 120 words per minute (wpm)	You have difficulty with basic word recognition. Look for a reading skills or literacy program in your local area.
120 to 180 wpm	Your reading speed is below average. You will benefit from extra daily practice drilling and reading.
180 to 240 wpm	You are an average reader. You should make quick and immediate progress with adequate practice.
240 to 300 wpm	You are an above-average reader. Your reading rate is average for a college student.
300 to 600 wpm	Your reading rate is above-average for a college student.
Above 600 wpm	You are a superior reader, assuming that you remember a good deal of what you read.

In this course, you should aim to double your present reading speed or read more than 600 words per minute—whichever is the higher reading rate!

My goals:

What would I like to be able to do after this program that I am currently not accomplishing?

- 600 wpm
- comprehension
- better spelling
- more reading

What Slows Us Down?

The basic reasons for slow reading are:

1. Reading one word at a time.

2. Regressions.

3. Subvocalizing.

The Evelyn Wood Reading Dynamics program is designed to overcome these barriers and allows you to read at speeds you didn't know were possible.

<u>**What You Need for This Lesson:**</u>

Evelyn Wood Course Guide

Audio CD #1

Pencil or pen

An easy novel or biography of your choice

Lesson 2

*Increase Your Reading
Speed Immediately*

The Underlining Hand Movement

1. Point your index finger and tuck your other fingers loosely under your thumb. If you're right-handed, use your right hand. If you're left-handed, use your left hand.

2. Place your index finger under the first word at the top left of the page.

3. Run the tip of your finger underneath the line of print, reading above your finger as you go.

4. At the end of the line, lift your finger slightly and bring it quickly back to the beginning of the next line.

1. Point index finger.

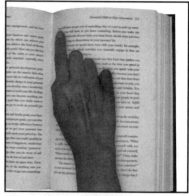

2. Place finger under first word.

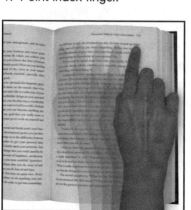

3. Run finger across line as you read.

4. Return to the start of the next line.

Upside-Down Drill

I was so frustrated by my own slow reading that I determined to teach myself to read faster and better, then try to teach high school students what I had learned to do for myself. I studied the reading authorities and I became confused. The educational literature contains such references as: In the May 1950 issue of Education, Elizabeth Simpson is quoted as saying, "Of course, no one would assume that while the tachistoscopic studies show we can recognize a word at 1/100th of a second, it is also true we can read 6,000 words in a minute. We know we can't recognize so many ideas so quickly." I began to think—what if the 6,000 words represented only one or two ideas? Would this make a difference? It is in the field where we know things can't be done that so much is being done. Nila Banton Smith, in her book, Read Faster, page 244, says, "We fixate at a point along the line and see all the words we can see to the left and right of the fixation, then move on to another fixation and repeat the perception process." Then she adds this observation: "But it happens that we also possess a vertical field of vision which usually lies dormant insofar as reading is concerned." I wondered why someone didn't do something to explore the

W-A-T-E-R

by Lorena A. Hickock

The day had got off to a bad start. It was April 5th, just two days over a month since The Stranger had come to be Helen's teacher.

Because Captain Keller had insisted on it, Helen and The Stranger had moved out of the cottage. He wanted his little girl at home. Now he and Helen's mother were learning the manual alphabet. But Captain Keller wasn't trying very hard.

"What's the use?" he kept saying.

"You're going to need it," The Stranger told him. "Sooner or later— and I believe it will be before very long—Helen will know the meaning of words. And then you can talk to her, with your fingers in her hand."

Helen was now much quieter and better behaved than she had been. Everybody noticed it. She did not have so many tantrums. And when she did have one, it did not last long. But sometimes, as on this April morning, she would wake up feeling out of sorts and cross. For one thing, she was getting bored with the word game.

"I know all that," she would think impatiently. "Why don't we play something else?"

All the morning The Stranger had been spelling two words into Helen's hand, W-A-T-E-R and C-U-P. She would spell C-U-P and give her a cup to hold. Then she would pour a little water into the cup, dip Helen's fingers into it, and wait hopefully for Helen to spell back W-A-T-E-R.

But Helen, not understanding, would spell C-U-P.

"What is it you want?" she kept thinking. "I'd do it if I knew. But I don't know. Can't you see I'm trying?"

"Poor child, you're getting tired," The Stranger said as Helen jerked her hand away and nearly upset the cup. "Let's rest awhile. Here!"

And she handed her the new doll she had brought her from Boston. Helen played with the doll awhile, but she was thinking of the word game.

"What do you want?" she kept saying to herself. "Why can't I do it? I try and try!"

Presently The Stranger started in on the word game again. C-U-P. W-A-T-E-R. But Helen kept getting more and more mixed up and irritable. Finally she seized her doll and dashed it to the floor. Its head broke in half a dozen pieces.

With grim satisfaction, she followed with her hands The Stranger's motions as she swept up the broken pieces.

"I don't care!" Helen told herself fiercely. "I don't care the least little bit! Why don't you leave me alone?"

She gave a little sigh of relief when The Stranger brought her hat to her. They were going outdoors. No more of that stupid game

.

Although Helen did not know it, The Stranger carried the cup in her hand as they walked down the path toward the pump house.

Helen raised her head and sniffed with pleasure. That sweet smell! Although she didn't know the word for it, it was honeysuckle. She reached out her hand and touched the vine lovingly as they passed.

Someone was pumping water. The Stranger led Helen to the pump, placed the cup in her hand again, and held it under the spout.

Helen's first impulse was to throw the cup away. But she liked the sensation as the cool water flowed down over her hand into the cup. So she held it there, smiling a little.

The Stranger took hold of her other hand and began to spell the word again. W-A-T-E-R. Slowly at first. Then faster. Over and over again.

Suddenly Helen dropped the cup. She stood absolutely still, rigid, hardly breathing. Inside her mind, a new thought spun round and round:

"W-A-T-E-R! W-A-T-E-R! This lovely, cool stuff. W-AT-E-R!"

Wildly she groped for The Stranger's hand. Her trembling little fingers began, W-A-T—? She had not finished when she felt The Stranger's pat of approval on her shoulder. She was right!

That was it!

For the first time in her life, Helen Keller had "talked" with another human being!

The Stranger's eyes were wet as she cried: "Helen, you've got it! You've got it!"

Helen could not hear her. But that did not matter. For now another idea came flashing into her mind.

If that stuff was W-A-T-E-R, what about the other games they played with their hands?

She reached down and touched the ground, then turned eagerly to The Stranger. Her heart pounding like a little hammer, she felt The Stranger's fingers moving in her hand.

Several times The Stranger's fingers spelled the word, Helen intently following every movement. Then she spelled it back. G-R-O-UN-D. She had it fixed in her memory now. She would not forget.

Now she must find out about more things, fast! She ran about, touching everything she could reach. The Stranger's fingers told her V-I-N-E,

P-U-M-P, T-R-E-L-L-I-S. Helen bumped into the nurse, who was coming into the pump house carrying Helen's baby sister, Mildred, whom she still thought of as "It." She touched "It" and ran back to The Stranger, B-AB-Y! It had been spelled into her hand many, many times. Now it had meaning. Little Mildred was no longer just a thing called "It."

Suddenly Helen stood still, thinking hard. Then she reached out toward The Stranger.

Although she could not put it into words, as you or I would, her hand grasping The Stranger's hand asked a question:

"Who are you?"

And into her eager little palm the word came back: T-E-A-C-H-E-R.

In that warm, glowing moment all the hostility Helen had felt toward The Stranger melted away. For no longer was she a stranger. She was Teacher.

T-E-A-C-H-E-R! To Helen Keller, the most important word she would ever learn. And to Anne Sullivan, the most beautiful.

This passage may be used to practice the Extension Drill.

How to Compute Your Rate

A. Add the total number of words on any three full lines of your book.	
B. Divide the total (A) by three, to find the average words per line.	
C. Count the total number of lines that you read in one minute.	
D. Multiply the answers of B times C, or the average number of words per line times the number of lines that you read.	WPM

EXAMPLE FROM "W-A-T-E-R":

A. Total number of words on three full lines	22
B. Divide A by three.	7
C. Total number of lines read	31
D. Multiply B times C.	217 WPM

A. Total number of words on three full lines	
B. Divide A by three.	
C. Total number of lines read	
D. Multiply B times C.	WPM

A. Total number of words on three full lines	
B. Divide A by three.	
C. Total number of lines read	
D. Multiply B times C.	WPM

Supplemental Practice

It is very important that you use your hand as a pacer for as much of your daily reading as possible. As with any habit, the more you practice, the quicker it becomes a useful, comfortable habit.

• Read at least one hour before Lesson Three, using your hand as a pacer. Read any book or magazine of your choice; it need not be done in one sitting.

• Practice the Extension Drill at least four times before going on to Lesson Three.

Extension Drill

1.   From any beginning point, read for one minute. Mark your ending point. Compute your rate.

     Note: To time yourself, use a timer or set a watch with a sweep second hand near your book or magazine.

2.   Reread the same material for one minute, read faster and farther. Mark your book or magazine.

3.   Reread the same material for one minute, read even faster and farther. Mark your new ending point.

4.   Reread the same material for one minute, read faster and even farther. Mark your new ending point.

5.   In new material, read for one minute for good comprehension. Mark your ending point, and compute your rate.

     Use the table on the next page to track your progress.

Practice Report Register

This is a weekly report of your progress at daily practice drills. With practice you will notice mprovement in your reading rate from day to day and week to week. Make it your goal to attempt ever increasing rates.

First Time	Time spent on drill: _____ mins.	Range of reading rates: ____ to ____ low high	Comments
Second Time	Time spent on drill: _____ mins.	Range of reading rates: ____ to ____ low high	Comments
Third Time	Time spent on drill: _____ mins.	Range of reading rates: ____ to ____ low high	Comments
Fourth Time	Time spent on drill: _____ mins.	Range of reading rates: ____ to ____ low high	Comments

Practice Summary
Record on your Progress Report Chart.

Total Time Spent on Drills: _____

Highest Reading Rate: _____

What You Need for This Lesson:

Evelyn Wood Course Guide

Audio CD #2

Pencil or pen

An easy novel or biography of your choice

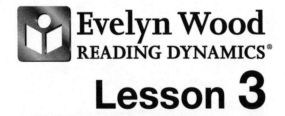

Evelyn Wood
READING DYNAMICS®

Lesson 3

Double Your Reading Speed

"Take Over Bos'n"
by Oscar Schisgall

Hour after hour I kept the gun pointed at the other nine men. From the lifeboat's stern, where I'd sat most of the twenty days of our drifting, I could keep them all covered. If I had to shoot at such close quarters, I wouldn't miss. They realized that. Nobody jumped at me, but in the way all glared, I could see how they had come to hate my guts. Especially Barrett, who'd been Bos'n's mate; Barrett said in his harsh, cracked voice, "You're half asleep now!" I didn't answer. He was right. How long can a man stay awake? I hadn't shut my eyes in maybe seventy-two hours. Very soon

now
I'd
doze
off,
and
the
instant
that
happened
they'd
pounce
on the
little
water
that
was
left.
The
last
canteen
lay
under
my legs.
There
wasn't
much
in it
after
twenty days.
Maybe a

pint. Enough
to give
each of us
a few drops.
Yet I
could see
in their
bloodshot eyes
that they'd
gladly kill
me for
those few
drops. As
a man
I didn't
count any
more. I
was no
longer third
officer of
the wrecked
Montala. It
was just
a gun
that kept
them away
from the
water they
craved. And
with their

cheeks sunken,
they were
half crazy.
The way
I judged
it, we
must be
some two
hundred miles
east of
Ascension.
The storms
were over the
Atlantic
swells, long
and easy,
and the
morning sun
was hot—
so hot
it scorched
your skin.
My own
tongue was
thick enough
to clog
my throat.
I'd have
given the
rest of

my life for a single gulp of water, but I was the man with the gun — the only authority in the boat — and I knew this: Once the water was gone, we'd have nothing to look forward to but death. As long as we could look forward to a drink later, there was something to live for. We had to make it last as long as possible. If I'd given in to the curses and growls, if I hadn't brandished the gun, we'd have emptied the last canteen days ago. By now we'd all be dead. The men weren't pulling on the oars. They'd stopped that long ago, too weak to go on. The nine of them facing me were a pack of bearded, ragged, half-naked animals, and I probably looked as the rest. Some sprawled over the gunwales dozing.

The rest watched as Barrett did, ready to spring the instant that I relaxed. When they weren't looking at my face they looked at the canteen under my legs. Jeff Barrett was the nearest one. A constant threat. The Bos'n's mate was a heavy man, bald, with a scarred and brutal face. He'd been in a hundred fights, and they'd left their marks on him. Barrett had been able to sleep — in fact, he'd slept through most of the night—and I envied him that. His eyes wouldn't close. They kept watching me, narrow and dangerous. Every now and then he taunted me in that hoarse, broken voice: "Why don't you quit? You can't hold out!" "Tonight," I said. "We'll ration the rest of the water tonight." "By tonight some of us'll be dead! We want it now!" "Tonight, " I said. Couldn't he understand that if we waited until night the few drops wouldn't be sweated out of us so fast? Barrett was beyond all reasoning. His mind had already cracked with thirst. I saw him begin to rise, a calculating look in his eyes. I aimed the gun at his chest and he sat down again. I'd grabbed my Luger on instinct twenty days ago just before running for the lifeboat. Nothing else would have kept Barrett and the rest away from the water. These fools, couldn't they see I wanted a drink as badly as any of them? But, I was in command here—that was the difference. I was the man with the gun who had to think. Each of the others could afford to think only of himself; I had to think of them all. Barrett's eyes kept watching me, waiting. I hated him. I hated him all the more because he slept. He had that advantage now. He wouldn't keel over. And long before noon I knew I couldn't fight any more. My eyelids were too heavy to lift. As the boat rose and fell on the long swells, I could feel sleep creeping over me like paralysis. It bent my head. It filled my brain like a cloud. I was going, going... Barrett stood over me, and I couldn't even lift the gun. In a vague way I could guess what could happen. He'd grab the water first to take his gulp. By that time the others would be screaming and tearing at him, and he'd have to yield the canteen. Well, there was nothing more I could do about it. I whispered, "Take over Bos'n." Then I fell face down in the bottom of the boat. I was asleep before I stopped moving. When a hand shook my shoulder, I could hardly raise my head. Jeff Barrett's hoarse voice said, "Here, take your share of the water!" Somehow I propped myself up

on my arms
dizzy and weak,
I looked at the
men, and I thought
my eyes were going.
Their figures were
dim and shadowy but
then I realized it
wasn't because of
my eyes. It was
night. The sea
was black; there
were stars overhead.
I'd slept the day away.
So we were in our
twenty-first night
adrift—the night
in which the tramp
Groton finally
picked us up.
I turned my head
to Barrett. There
was no sign of
any ship. He knelt
beside me, holding
out the canteen,
his other hand
with the gun
steady on the
men. I stared at

the canteen as
if it were a
mirage. Hadn't they
finished that pint
of water this
morning? When I
looked up at
Barrett's ugly
face, it was
grim. He must
have guessed my
thoughts. "You said,
'Take over, Bos'n,'
didn't you?" he
growled. "I been
holdin' off these
apes all day."
He lifted the
Luger in his
hand. "When you're
boss-man," he
added with a
sheepish grin, "in
command and
responsible for
the rest,
you sure
get to see
things different,
don't you?"

"Take Over Bos'n" Quiz

1. The officer in charge carried what kind of weapon?

2. The boat had been drifting for how many days?

3. The bos'n mate's name was…

4. The officer in charge had been awake for how many hours?

5. What was the approximate location of the drifting boats?

6. What was the weather like?

7. How many men faced the officer in charge?

8. What did the men want so desperately?

9. Describe the appearance of the men in the boat.

10. When the officer keeled over, what did the bos'n's mate do?

Supplemental Practice

Practice using your hand as a pacer as much of the time as possible. Complete the following assignments before going on to Lesson Four:

• Read at least one hour before Lesson Four, using your hand as a pacer. This reading may be done in any book or magazine of your choice, and it need not be done all in one sitting.

• Practice the Push-Down Drill at least four times before going on to Lesson Four.

Push-Down Drill

1. From any beginning point, read for one minute. Mark your ending point, and compute your rate.

2. Reread the same material in 50 seconds. Strive to make your mark.

3. Reread the same material in 40 seconds, making your mark.

4. Practice read the same section in 30 seconds, making the mark.

5. Practice read the same section in 25 seconds, making the mark.

6. Practice read the same section in 20 seconds, making the mark.

7. From the end of the section that you've been practicing, read new material as fast as you can with good comprehension. You have one minute. Mark your ending point, and compute your rate.

   Use the table on the next page to track your progress.

Practice Report Register

This is a weekly report of your progress at daily practice drills. Ideally, you should see an improvement in rate from day to day and week to week. Make it your goal to attempt ever increasing rates.

First Time	Time spent on drill: _____ mins.	Range of reading rates: ____ to ____ low high	Comments
Second Time	Time spent on drill: _____ mins.	Range of reading rates: ____ to ____ low high	Comments
Third Time	Time spent on drill: _____ mins.	Range of reading rates: ____ to ____ low high	Comments
Fourth Time	Time spent on drill: _____ mins.	Range of reading rates: ____ to ____ low high	Comments

Practice Summary
Record on your Progress Report Chart.

Total Time Spent on Drills: _____

Highest Reading Rate: _____

What You Need for This Lesson:

Evelyn Wood Course Guide

Audio CD #2

Pencil or pen

Blank paper, lined or unlined

A book of your choice, fiction or nonfiction

Lesson 4

**Remember More of
What You Read**

Slash Recall Pattern

Directions: On the main diagonal line, answer the question, "What is it about?" On branch lines, add supporting items and details. Add branches if you need them.

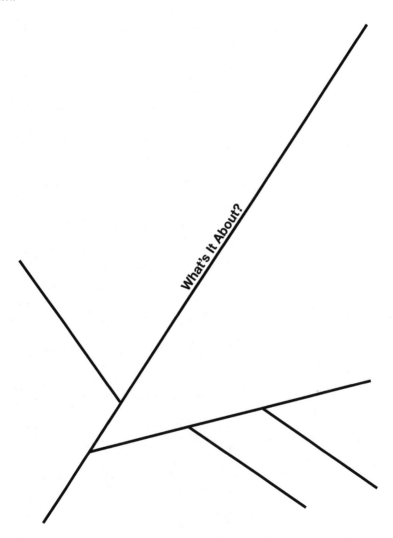

What's It About?

Sample Slash Recall Pattern for "Goldilocks and the Three Bears"

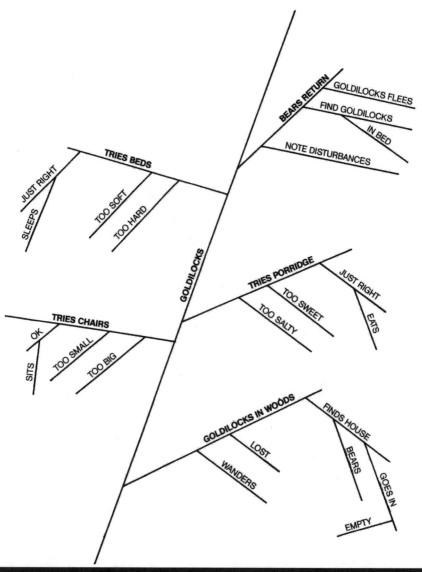

Slash Recall Pattern

Directions: On the main diagonal line, answer the question, "What is it about?" On branch lines, add supporting items and details. Add branches if you need them.

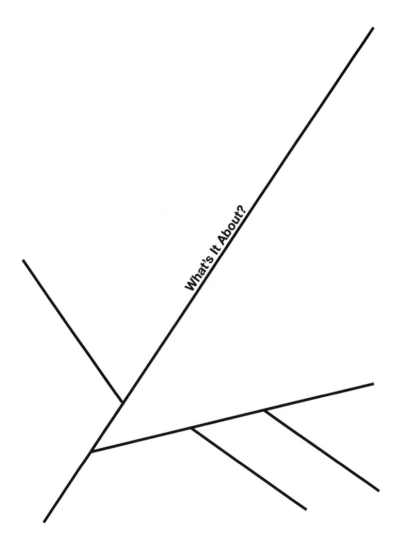

Main diagonal line label: What's It About?

Slash Recall Pattern

Directions: On the main diagonal line, answer the question, "What is it about?" On branch lines, add supporting items and details. Add branches if you need them.

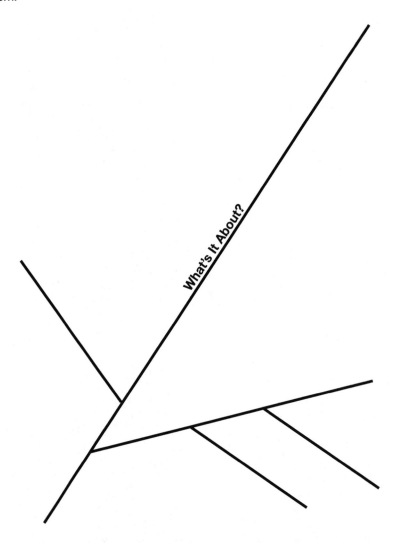

What's It About?

Supplemental Practice

In addition to using your hand as a pacer for as much of your daily reading as possible, also make Slash Recall Patterns for as many readings as you can in order to develop the habit of immediate recall. Complete the following assignments before going on to Lesson Five:

- Read at least one hour before Lesson Five, using your hand as a pacer. This reading may be done in any book of your choice, and it need not be done all at one sitting.

- Practice the Add Half a Page Drill at least four times before going on to Lesson Five.

Add Half a Page Drill

1. From any beginning point, read for one minute. Mark your ending point with a number 1, and compute your rate.

2. Put a number 2 one-half page ahead; go back to the same starting point above, and practice reading to the 2 in one minute. Be sure to make your mark.

3. Put a number 3 one-half page ahead; go back to the same starting point above, and practice reading to the 3 in one minute. Be sure to make the mark.

4. Put a number 4 one-half page ahead; practice reading this larger section in one minute, making your mark.

5. Put a number 5 one-half page ahead; practice reading this larger section in one minute, making the mark.

6. Go back to the number 1 in your book, and read as far as you can for good comprehension for one minute. Make an X mark where you stopped reading; make a Slash Recall Pattern; then go back and compute your rate.

Use the table on the next page to track your progress.

Practice Report Register

This is a weekly report of your progress at daily practice drills. Ideally, you should see an improvement in rate from day to day and week to week. Make it your goal to attempt ever increasing rates.

First Time	Time spent on drill: _____ mins.	Range of reading rates: ____ to ____ low high	Comments
Second Time	Time spent on drill: _____ mins.	Range of reading rates: ____ to ____ low high	Comments
Third Time	Time spent on drill: _____ mins.	Range of reading rates: ____ to ____ low high	Comments
Fourth Time	Time spent on drill: _____ mins.	Range of reading rates: ____ to ____ low high	Comments

Practice Summary
Record on your Progress Report Chart.

Total Time Spent on Drills: _____

Highest Reading Rate: _____

What You Need for This Lesson:

Evelyn Wood Course Guide

Audio CD #3

Pencil or pen

Blank paper

A book of your choice, fiction or nonfiction

Evelyn Wood
READING DYNAMICS®

Lesson 5

Push for Greater Reading Rates

"Shaky" Hand Movement Practice

I was so frustrated by my own slow reading that I determined to teach myself to read faster and better, then try to teach high school students what I had learned to do for myself. I studied the reading authorities and I became confused. The educational literature contains such references as: In the May 1950 issue of Education, Elizabeth Simpson is quoted as saying, "Of course, no one would assume that while the tachistoscopic studies show we can recognize a word at 1/100th of a second, it is also true we can read 6,000 words in a minute. We know we can't recognize so many ideas so quickly." I began to think—what if the 6,000 words represented only one or two ideas? Would this make a difference? It is in the field where we know things can't be done that so much is being done. Nila Banton Smith, in her book, Read Faster, page 244, says, "We fixate at a point along the line and see all the words we can see to the left and right of the fixation, then move on to another fixation and repeat the perception process." Then she adds this observation: "But it happens that we also possess a vertical field of vision which usually lies dormant insofar as reading is concerned." I wondered why someone didn't do something to explore the potentialities of this field.

Supplemental Practice

Use your hand as a pacer for all your daily reading. Complete the following assignments before going on to Lesson Six:

- Read at least one hour before Lesson Six, using your hand as a pacer. This reading may be done in any book or magazine of your choice, and it need not be done all at one sitting.

- Do the Push-Up Drill at least four times before going on to the next lesson.

Push-Up Drill

1. Read from a beginning point for one minute for good comprehension. Mark your ending point, and compute your rate. Optional: Begin a Slash Recall Pattern.

2. Reread the same material for one minute; try to go farther. Make a new mark if you read farther ahead and erase the former one. Optional: Add to your Slash Recall Pattern.

3. Reread the same material again for one minute; go farther still. Make a new mark if you read farther ahead and erase the former one. Optional: Add to your Slash Recall Pattern.

4. Set up a second section of material immediately after and approximately equal to the amount covered in number 3. Practice read both sections in one minute. You must make the mark!

5. Set up a third section of material approximately equal to the section set up in number 4. Practice read all three sections in one minute. Make the mark!

6. Read new material for one minute for good comprehension. Make a mark where you stopped reading, and compute your rate. Optional: Add to your Slash Recall Pattern.

Use the table on the next page to track your progress

Practice Report Register

This is a weekly report of your progress at daily practice drills. Ideally, you should see an improvement in rate from day to day and week to week. Make it your goal to attempt ever increasing rates.

First Time	Time spent on drill: _____ mins.	Range of reading rates: ____ to ____ low high	Comments
Second Time	Time spent on drill: _____ mins.	Range of reading rates: ____ to ____ low high	Comments
Third Time	Time spent on drill: _____ mins.	Range of reading rates: ____ to ____ low high	Comments
Fourth Time	Time spent on drill: _____ mins.	Range of reading rates: ____ to ____ low high	Comments

Practice Summary
Record on your Progress Report Chart.

Total Time Spent on Drills: _____

Highest Reading Rate: _____

What You Need for This Lesson:

Evelyn Wood Course Guide

Audio CD #3

Pencil or pen

Blank paper

A newspaper of your choice (optional)

Evelyn Wood
READING DYNAMICS®

Lesson 6

Read the Newspaper More Efficiently

Proposed Budget Expected to Meet With Opposition

When Mayor Marc LaFrette presents his proposed budget to the City Council today, he isn't likely to be the most popular guy in town. LaFrette's budget will reverse a 10-year trend of reducing, or at least capping, property taxes.

Ten years ago, voters overwhelmingly approved a referendum requiring property tax revenue could not grow more than 3 percent a year.

In order to comply with the referendum, the tax rate would have to be reduced about a half mil, translating to about $24 million in revenue. This revenue is needed for city services such as police and fire protection. "It would be irresponsible to continue down this road of reducing revenue while our population is in such a growth phase," said Rose Blankenship, public relations director for the city.

So how will the mayor get around the referendum? A legal team of advisors argues that referendums are not legally binding.

But while he may win a legal battle, he may lose the popular opinion battle. "What's the point in voting for

something if they can just ignore it!" argued Northside resident Rodney Grant.

The previous two mayors chose to stick with the referendum.

LaFrette campaigned heavily on making the government more efficient. Many opponents argue that LaFrette should focus on cutting unnecessary waste, rather than raising the tax revenue. "Raising taxes is the easy way out!" says Jeremy Blanchard, who opposed LaFrette in last year's election. "Anyone can raise taxes, but it takes a real leader to manage expenses while still providing a strong quality of life to residents."

While the budget will be presented today, the City Council is not expected to vote on it for two weeks.

The proposed budget will still have a reduction in the millage rate, but will only save the average household about $5 a year.

Historically, voters have not responded well to ignored referendums. Former Mayor Sandra Myers lost a reelection bid after a fierce battle with political newcomer James Stockton. Analysts suggest that Myers' changes to the school funding referendum cost her that election.

Holiday Cheer Hurts Job Seekers

In a season of shopping, packages, parties, and festivities, Chester Smith isn't feeling very jolly. Out of work since September, Smith says employment opportunities have dried up since the beginning of the holiday season.

"I was finding two or three jobs every week to apply for," Smith comments. "Since Thanksgiving, I'm lucky if I find even one a week."

Smith's experience isn't unusual. According to the Department of Labor, hiring activity is down across the country.

Analysts say it isn't a sign of a downturn in the economy, but rather a yearly cycle that is quite common. "We often see a dip in recruitment and hiring activity from mid-November through mid-January," comments Janice Franssen of Franssen and Associates, a headhunting firm based in Charlotte.

According to Franssen, this period of inactivity is followed by one of the most active times of the year when hiring is at its peak from mid-January to mid-February. The January surge can be attributed to new funding available at the first of the year, and making up for lost time. "Employers are often scrambling to fill positions that they didn't have time to deal with over the holidays," according to Franssen.

This may not bring too much comfort to job seekers like Smith. "Two months is a long time to wait for the job market to pick up, especially when the kids are still expecting Christmas presents!"

The current unemployment rate is lower than this time last year, providing some hope to those still looking.

Employment is actually at its highest for the year in the retail, food service, and travel industries. "We're hiring people on the spot in some cases," observes Francis McDonough, general manager at the Wine Reserve Restaurant and Event Center. "We are booked solid for the next four weeks and can use all the help we can get."

Economic indicators for next year's job growth are mixed. Early reports on consumer spending for the holiday season are positive, yet rising oil prices and interest rates are likely to keep growth from being too strong.

"But I'm still out there—I'm still trying," promises Smith with a smile.

Early Birds Get a Jump on Hurricane Preparation

With hurricane season just around the corner, it is a good time to take stock of just how prepared you are.

"The best time to prepare for a storm is now," advises Chip Johnson of the Emergency Planning Council. "By the time you see a storm on the news, you are already at a disadvantage."

Last year's hurricane season provided proof. Long lines at grocery stores and home improvement retailers were common sights throughout the state. With a little planning, that could have been avoided, says Johnson.

With another active season predicted, Johnson recommends the following steps to make sure you are prepared.

Check your disaster supply kit to make sure it is complete and current. Check expiration dates on food items and medicine that may have been sitting around for a few years. Look for items that have to be replenished after last year's storms. "And don't forget to think about the growth of your family," recommends Johnson. "Last year, I talked to several families who thought they were prepared because they had a box in the garage from several years ago. They hadn't taken their new baby into account and were in a sticky situation when they ran out of diapers in the middle of the storm."

Make insurance claims easier to process by creating a file with insurance policies, receipts for big-ticket items, and photos or a video of the contents of your house. Keep all this information in a portable, waterproof container in case you are faced with flooding or evacuation.

Create an evacuation plan for your family. Know what flood zone you are in and what the recommended evacuation routes are best for your area. Make advanced arrangements with friends or relatives who live inland in case you need to get away. Be sure to think about family pets as well. "Finding a hotel, shelter, or friend that will take your two large dogs might make things difficult," warns Johnson. "A little planning in advance can alleviate that hassle."

Make a checklist and gather supplies to prepare your house for the storm. Because storms can change direction quickly, you may not have a lot of time to prepare your house. A checklist, assigned duties, and adequate supplies on hand can make the process smooth and quick.

"Fortunately, a hurricane is one of the most polite natural disasters," jokes Johnson. "You know they are coming and you usually have a few days notice." But if everyone is waiting to prepare in those few days, it can become a real nightmare. "That's why I like to prepare, so I can sit in my easy chair, ready for the storm, watching all the procrastinators on the news standing in line."

Supplemental Practice

Use your hand as a pacer for all your daily reading. Complete the following assignments before going on to Lesson Seven:

- Read at least one hour before Lesson Seven, using your hand as a pacer. This reading may be done in any book or magazine of your choice, and it need not be done all at one sitting.

- Do the Newspaper Reading Drill given below at least four times before going on to the next lesson.

- Optional: Do the Push-Up Drill from the last lesson four times before going on to Lesson Seven.

Newspaper Reading Drill

1.   Look at only the headlines of the front page and any other favorite pages, such as the sports page or business page. If there is a summary of the day's news, read that.

2.   Decide from step one what you wish to read in 10 minutes. If there is no news summary, then quickly thumb through the entire paper, just looking at headlines and deciding what you will read.

3.   Beginning at the front page, read as quickly as you can just those articles you have decided to read. Read only as far in the article as you need to fulfill your purpose in reading it. Stop at the end of 10 minutes.

4.   Roughly calculate how many pages you covered in 10 minutes. Each day try to cover more pages.

Use the table on the next page to track your progress

Practice Report Register

This is a weekly report of your progress at daily practice drills. Ideally, you should see an improvement in rate from day to day and week to week. Make it your goal to attempt ever increasing rates.

First Time	Time spent on drill: _____ mins.	Range of reading rates: ____ to ____ low high	Comments
Second Time	Time spent on drill: _____ mins.	Range of reading rates: ____ to ____ low high	Comments
Third Time	Time spent on drill: _____ mins.	Range of reading rates: ____ to ____ low high	Comments
Fourth Time	Time spent on drill: _____ mins.	Range of reading rates: ____ to ____ low high	Comments

Practice Summary
Record on your Progress Report Chart.

Total Time Spent on Drills: _____

Highest Reading Rate: _____

<u>**What You Need for This Lesson:**</u>

Evelyn Wood Course Guide

Audio CD #4

Pencil or pen

Blank paper

A book of your choice, preferably a nonfiction book you haven't read or haven't read in a while.

Evelyn Wood
READING DYNAMICS®

Lesson 7

**Develop Better Reading
Comprehension**

The Multiple Reading Process

1. *Overview*

2. *Preview*

3. *Reading*

4. *Post-View*

Reading Forms and Techniques

FORM	ORGANIZATION	TECHNIQUE
News Articles	Inverted pyramid: title or headline, summary paragraphs, details in descending order of importance.	Preview by reading the summary paragraphs. Look over the rest of the article for unusual features.
Expository Writing *Nonfiction: textbooks, newspaper features, magazine articles*	Introduction of main idea, body, conclusion. Key information tends to lie at beginning and end of sections. Pattern repeats within subsections.	Preview by reading beginning and end of main section; look over whole for key ideas; also see beginning and end of key subsections.
Fiction *Short stories and novels*	Exposition of situation and characters; complication of the situation (sometimes leading to crises and a climax); resolution of the situation. This pattern tends to repeat within chapters.	Preview by reading dust jacket, table of contents, preface. Preview by scanning to find the elements necessary for the story to take place: characters, setting, time.
Biography	Episodes in a person's life.	Preview by checking table of contents or chapter titles to see development of person's life.
Technical and Scientific Writing *Journals and reports*	Inverted pyramid: title, conclusion, summary. Most important data, balance in descending order of importance.	Preview by looking over organization, noting sections, photos, charts. Read summary, introduction, conclusion; look for unusual features.

The Myth of the Overworked Executive
by Clarence B. Randall

A fine automobile is one of the miracles of modern engineering. Beneath the hood lies unlimited power, ready to lunge into immediate action at the slightest touch of the accelerator. Yet there is no unseemly outward manifestation of that power. Stand beside the car when the engine is running, and you scarcely hear a sound. There is no observable movement or vibration.

You cannot see the brakes, but they are wondrously efficient. The power can easily be released, but it can instantly be brought back under control. The car is always on the alert, always ready to do its job, but it is constructed for easy guidance and complete control at all times.

We have fine business executives who are like that. Their behavior is marked by outward calm and poise. Underneath lies tremendous personal capacity and power. Great effort is not signaled by outward commotion.

They can take decisive action without breaking through the barriers of orderly restraint. In the African jungle, the lion roars as he springs for the kill, but among executives, those who are the leaders can exert their greatest strength without lifting their voices.

I am not, however, writing of these men, but of their opposites.

In nearly every organization, there is a self-appointed overworked executive. All day, every day, he advertises his martyrdom. His, he believes, is the pivotal responsibility in his company. Constantly sorry for himself because of the enormous burden he bears, he calls all men to witness the sacrifices he makes for the good of the company, sacrifices so little appreciated by his superior officers. Privately and yet to all who will listen, he pours out his personal woe, which is that he is badly underpaid.

Here is how you will know him: His desk is a mess. Papers are strewn across it in wild disarray, creating the impression that every important corporate transaction comes to him for approval. Yet, if you should discreetly make a few spotchecks, you would find that many of the letters and memos that he paws through to find the one you are after were there last week. They will be there next week, too. Should you find one day, to your surprise, a slight improvement, you would probably later discover that he achieved this in desperation by sweeping an armful of papers into the desk drawer.

Close by our hero's elbow is a large ashtray, half full of partly smoked cigarettes, to indicate the extreme nervous tension under which he operates.

He seldom goes out to lunch, but has a sandwich and a glass of milk brought in. This adds to the buildup. Not a moment of his time must be lost, or earnings for the month will go off sharply.

In his hand when he leaves the office is the inevitable bulging briefcase. He would no more be caught without that mark of martyrdom than he would be seen without his trousers. True, many of the papers in it have already made a great many round trips without being disturbed. But, nevertheless, this nightly show makes it clear to all that here is a very important man.

When finally he bursts in the front door of his house, he pecks his wife hastily on the cheek and expects to sit down at the table immediately. He must never be kept waiting. He has dropped his briefcase in the front hall, where it is likely to stay till morning if there should happen to be a night ball game on. At best it will be a tug-of-war between the papers and the blare of television for several hours.

There will be little general family conversation.

One of this man's proudest boasts is that he has not had a vacation in 10 years. "Just can't take the time," he says. That his wife deserves one, and that his family is growing up without the joy of experiences shared with him, are considerations outside his realm of understanding. Actually, his capacity for enjoyment is so atrophied that he would not know what to do with a vacation if forced into it. Nonetheless, he will soon have one involuntarily —in a hospital—when his coronary thrombosis comes, as it surely will.

He is greatly given to travel, rushing about on planes, briefcase in hand, as though the number of miles flown in a year were any criterion of effective effort. Physical activity gives him a proud sense of doing. Often a long distance call, if prudently planned and intelligently carried through, would fully answer the purpose; but that would somehow downgrade the whole transaction. Nor does he ever achieve much by correspondence, since he has never learned to express himself cogently and persuasively in a letter.

What little responsibility he bears he shares with no one. To simplify his day by delegating to juniors the routine clerical part of his tasks would deflate his ego. Neither superior officer nor associate is ever quite sure just what it is that occupies him so intensively. If something takes him away from his desk, whether for an hour or for a week, everything stops.

Partly this is because it gives him satisfaction to surround himself with a slight air of mystery. For example, he is highly secretive about his personal affairs. He would not think of letting a secretary handle his checkbook or take his deposits to the bank. She might find out how small his income really is in comparison with the image he is endeavoring to create.

He has never had a will drawn, has never had a frank talk with his wife as to what to do or whom to consult in case of his death, or told her what she may expect by way of income during her remaining years. His meager insurance policies are not collected in one place, and his social security card is long since lost.

He is chronically late for all engagements. When a staff conference is called, he bustles into the room 15 minutes after it has been begun, wearing an air of preoccupation that is intended to suggest to his colleagues that it is generous indeed for a man who bears such manifest responsibility to take time for such lesser matters at all.

In his office he keeps visitors waiting beyond the time set for the engagement, partly because his awareness of his surroundings is so low that he is actually not conscious of the passage of time, and partly because by delaying others he reminds himself once more of his own importance.

The presence of such a disordered life within an organization can have repercussions that are the very antithesis of good management. Inevitably, this man becomes a focal point from which confusion and uncertainty spread. Policy is neither reliably implemented by such an individual nor accurately transmitted to others. Because he cannot discipline himself, he can neither lead nor discipline others.

The fault lies within. What is missing is the inner poise and deep humility that come from the continuous development of the adult mind and spirit.

A person of this type is almost invariably one who early abandoned the cultivation of the mind. Yet, sadly enough, he is more often than not a college graduate. He has no intellectual satisfactions. From one year's end to the next, he never enters into the companionship of great minds by good reading. He confines himself strictly to the daily paper, principally the financial and sporting sections, and to his trade journals. He hears no concerts, attends no art exhibits, participates in no discussion groups. He has no views on the questions of the day other than a continuing stream of verbose invective directed toward all those in authority.

In the realm of the spirit, he possesses no basic philosophy to which he may turn in times of stress. He has no sense of values that find expression in his life from day to day, values that others come to recognize and respect. Yet mental serenity and internal resources are never lacking in the truly great executives of American industry. They must, of course, have fine minds and strong wills. But the power of their personalities finds expression through order and a self-discipline so immaculate that it is seldom apparent as a separable trait of character.

When a visitor is shown in to a good executive, he finds before him a clean desk and behind it a man who is at ease, who makes him feel that this is the call he has been waiting for, and who listens attentively. Yet, subtly, the man behind the desk is in control of the interview all of the time and knows how to terminate it without giving offense.

The good executive also has a plan for his day. He knows what things have to be accomplished if the required tempo is to be maintained, and times himself accordingly. With deliberate speed he moves from one task to the next, making his decisions resolutely when he senses the matter has consumed the maximum period that can be allotted to it. There is no outward sign of inner struggle, and the job gets done.

He works a full day, though not an overly long one. When the normal quitting time comes, except for those sudden emergencies that no man can control, he will walk promptly out of office with a sense of satisfaction at what he has accomplished. And in closing the door, he will put it all behind him. His evenings and his weekends bring him a change of pace. In company with his family and neighbors, he turns with high enthusiasm to other challenging interests that are totally unrelated to his daily routines. When he comes back to his job, both his body and his mind have been refreshed.

His ideas do not become inbred, because he spends a great deal of time with people who know nothing whatever about his business and who are not particularly impressed with his responsibilities. Many of them do not even know what he does, and care less. This helps him keep his own importance in perspective.

He has a zest for vacations. He knows that rotation of interests is as important to the productivity of the mind as rotation of crops is to the fertility of the soil.

He has the excellent characteristic of laughing well. His lively and infectious sense of humor lubricates all of his human relationships.

In short, the self-pitying, overworked executive is a man who presses badly. The fine executive is one who always takes a free, easy swing at the ball.

Supplemental Practice

Use your hand as a pacer for all your daily reading. Do the following assignments before going on to Lesson Eight:

- Read at least one hour before Lesson Eight, using your hand as a pacer. This reading may be done in any book or magazine of your choice.

- Do the Dynamic Reading Drill employing the Multiple Reading Process, given below, at least four times before going on to the next lesson.

Dynamic Reading Drill

1. Select a chapter of about 10 pages (300 to 500 words per page) from an interesting book, preferably nonfiction.

2. Using the techniques learned in this lesson, preview the chapter as fast as you can—one to two minutes should be plenty of time. Find what the important points of the chapter are, so you can decide your reading purpose.

3. Read the chapter as fast as you can, keeping your purpose in mind. Speed up where comprehension comes easily; slow down where it is more difficult. Calculate your rate.

4. Decide if there is anything that you seem to be missing from the material, anything that you wish to clarify or check or just go over again. Then postview the section in one to two minutes with the goal of getting that information.

To compute a rate while reading a whole chapter:

A. Keep track of the total time used (in quarters of minutes)	
B. Compute the average words per page (rounded off)	
C. Multiply the words per page by the number of pages read.	
D. Divide the number of words by the amount of time used.	

Practice Report Register

This is a weekly report of your progress at daily practice drills. Ideally, you should see an improvement in rate from day to day and week to week. Make it your goal to attempt ever increasing rates.

First Time	Time spent on drill: _____ mins.	Range of reading rates: ____ to ____ low high	Comments
Second Time	Time spent on drill: _____ mins.	Range of reading rates: ____ to ____ low high	Comments
Third Time	Time spent on drill: _____ mins.	Range of reading rates: ____ to ____ low high	Comments
Fourth Time	Time spent on drill: _____ mins.	Range of reading rates: ____ to ____ low high	Comments

Practice Summary
Record on your Progress Report Chart.

Total Time Spent on Drills: _____

Highest Reading Rate: _____

What You Need for This Lesson:

Evelyn Wood Course Guide

Audio CD #4

Pencil or pen

Blank paper

A nonfiction book of your choice

Evelyn Wood
READING DYNAMICS®

Lesson 8

*Organize What You've
Read to Remember It*

How Organization Works

apples
dry cereal
sugar
pork chops
milk
butter
eggs
steak
toilet paper
glass
cleaner
bread

rice
peas
broccoli
chicken
macaroni
cheese
potatoes
green beans
lettuce
tomatoes
soft drinks
cucumbers

ice cream
carrots
shrimp
sour cream
flour
coffee
paper towels
spare ribs
spinach
hamburger
bacon
jam

cheesecake
beer
paper
napkins
cupcakes
tuna fish
cold cuts
cottage
cheese
steel wool
laundry soap
peaches

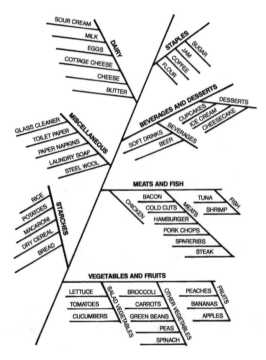

When the items are organized into groups of seven items or fewer, they are easier to remember than 46 single items.

Sample Slash Recall Pattern

Psychology Today
"Stages of Development"

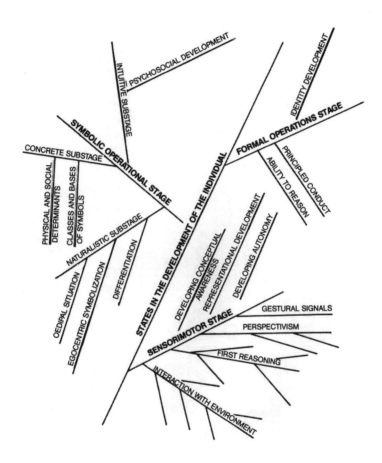

Sample "Spoke" Recall Pattern

The Old Man and the Sea
by Earnest Hemingway

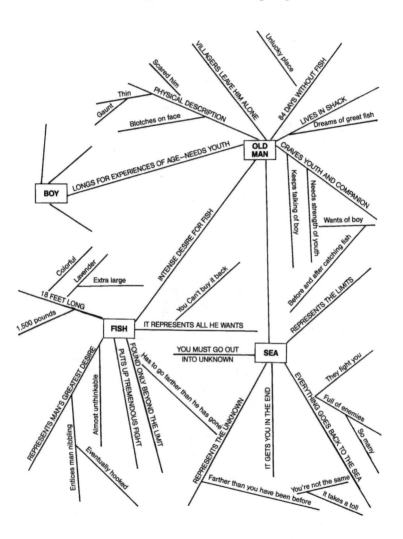

Sample Linear Recall

Legal Problems in Engineering

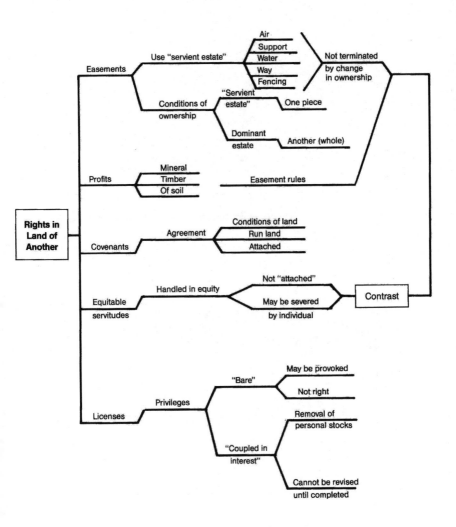

Sample Random Recall Patterns

Excellence
by John W. Gardner

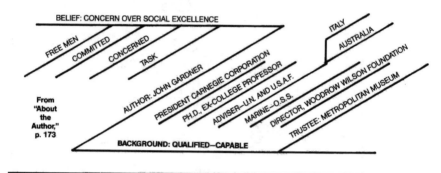

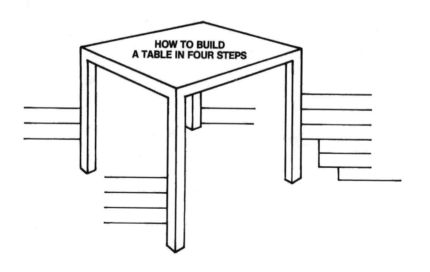

Ways to Improve Your Recall

1. Be selective when you read.

2. Develop a point of view toward the material; grasp its structure or theme.

3. Read with a definite purpose to satisfy an interest.

4. Organize as you read.

5. After reading, do something creative and useful with the information.

Supplemental Practice

Use your hand as a pacer for all your daily reading. Do the following assignments before you begin Lesson Nine:

- Read at least one hour before Lesson Nine, using your hand as a pacer. This reading may be done in any book or magazine of your choice, and it need not be done all at one sitting.

- Practice the Dynamic Reading Drill given below, using the Multiple Reading Process, at least four times before going on to the next lesson.

Dynamic Reading Drill

1. Select a chapter of approximately 10 pages from an interesting book of nonfiction.

2. Scan the whole chapter to locate subheads and any other signs of the author's organization of the material. Set up a Recall Pattern to reflect the organization.

3. Preview the chapter for its main ideas. Stop and add to your Recall Pattern as much of the preview information as you can remember.

4. Read the chapter as fast as you can. Stop and add to your Recall Pattern any additional information you can remember. Calculate your reading rate for the entire reading.

5. Post-view the chapter as fast as you can. Stop and add new information to your slash Recall Pattern.

Use the table on the next page to track your progress.

Practice Report Register

This is a weekly report of your progress at daily practice drills. Ideally, you should see an improvement in rate from day to day and week to week. Make it your goal to attempt ever increasing rates.

First Time	Time spent on drill: _____ mins.	Range of reading rates: ____ to ____ low high	Comments
Second Time	Time spent on drill: _____ mins.	Range of reading rates: ____ to ____ low high	Comments
Third Time	Time spent on drill: _____ mins.	Range of reading rates: ____ to ____ low high	Comments
Fourth Time	Time spent on drill: _____ mins.	Range of reading rates: ____ to ____ low high	Comments

Practice Summary
Record on your Progress Report Chart.

Total Time Spent on Drills: _____

Highest Reading Rate: _____

<u>**What You Need for This Lesson:**</u>

Evelyn Wood Course Guide

Audio CD #5

Pencil or pen

Blank paper

A textbook or nonfiction book of your choice

Lesson 9

Develop Dynamic Study Skills

Study Reading Techniques

For the book as a whole:	
Conduct an Overview	Overview the jacket or cover of the book, and read about the author and any other information. Examine the table of contents to understand the organization of the book.
For each chapter, analyze the whole:	
Overview	Inspect style, form, organization, and look over any maps, photos, illustrations, footnotes, etc.
Set Purpose	Use summaries and questions at the end to decide what you need from the material. What may be gained? What is essential?
Preview and Divide	Look over the whole, isolating where the necessary information lies, and divide the whole into manageable sections, according to your purpose.
Recall and Question	Set up a recall format with a place for each section. Create questions for each section.
For each section:	
Preview and Recall	Preview for main ideas only. In some cases, it will be necessary to first write down dates and other essentially structural information.
Read and Recall	Read for additional information to fill in main ideas. Check difficult areas that will require rereading or clarifying.
Reorganize the whole:	
Reorganize	Read checked material. Repeat until your purpose is met (until you can recall in your own words the necessary information).
Remember and Review	Reorganize the Recall Pattern; develop your own relationships and organization (book closed); do it in a new way.
	To review, reconstruct Recall Patterns from memory at regular intervals.

Example of a Study Recall Pattern

This Slash Recall Pattern is set up using the author's organization. This chapter is broken into three main parts (represented by the three main branches), and each part has as many sections as there are sub-branches. Some sections have subsections. After this is completed take each section or subsection to preview and recall, then read and recall, until your purpose is met—when you recall enough without looking at the material to feel that you really know it.

Psychology Today
"Stages of Development"

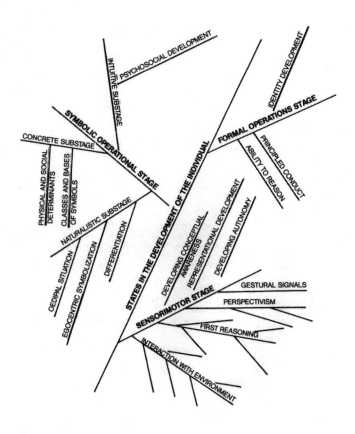

Reality of the People's Republic

by Claude Buss

Since 1949, China should be taken to mean the giant, complex nation-state in East Asia with the greatest population and the oldest continuing civilization in the world. Officially, China is called the People's Republic of China. It is the largest Communist country in the world.

The Land. Whatever China is called, it is larger than the United States, extending 2,000 miles from the north to the semitropical south; and nearly as great a distance from the China Seas on the east to the mountains and arid deserts of Central Asia on the west.

The geographic panorama is too varied for general description; each locality and each season is special. China possesses tremendous urban centers like Beijing, its capital, and Shanghai, Canton, Hankow, Tientsin, Harbin and Mukden. It also has many smaller urban areas with populations of more than 100,000 inhabitants, and a host of towns which we might regard as county seats.

The People. China's overall population is over 1.3 billion—the largest in the world. The majority of China's people still live in clusters of homes or villages and make their livelihood from agriculture.

The Culture. The Chinese have a sense of oneness which stems from their written language, common way of life, and Confucian tradition. Confucius was a contemporary of Socrates. His thought and philosophy, as interpreted by generations of disciples, have influenced the Chinese as much as the combined writings of the Greek philosophers and Christian theologians have shaped the intellectual life of the West.

An inextinguishable love of life and persistent sense of beauty have created a vital artistic tradition, while a high regard for the written word has given China a voluminous body of source materials. The country has been pursuing massive education programs, and there is a high degree of interest in all forms of literature.

Influence of the West. Along with its cultural tradition, China has inherited much of the political thought of the West. In the 19th century, the native way of life was shattered by the intrusion of Western merchants, missionaries, soldiers, and diplomats. Imperialism begat anti-imperialism and anti-imperialism begat revolution.

The Opium War of 1840 caused scarcely a stir in most of China, but the frightful T'ai P'ing rebellion (1854-1865) brought death to millions and spread destruction through a dozen provinces. Chinese conservatives were impotent to preserve the old order against the onslaught of new and modern ideas.

After China's defeat at the hands of Japan in 1894, China's great revolutionary, Sun Yat-sen, tried to rally his country against the decadent Manchu dynasty. His ideas gained immense support when, as a consequence of the Boxer Rebellion in 1900, a handful of foreign forces drove the imperial court out of the capital city. For the next decade, the Empress Dowager frantically tried to check the coming storm by building a new army and modernizing the political system. Her efforts were in vain. A revolution, which the Chinese now refer to as liberal democratic bourgeois revolution, broke out in 1911, and a Chinese republic replaced the ancient empire.

The republic, and the entire concept of popular government, got off to an unfortunate start in China. Those who espoused it were incompetent men. Civil authority gave way to warlords, and the poor suffered more than ever. Ideas of nationalism, democracy and social welfare grew in the minds of leaders sincerely desirous of putting an end to chaos. Sun Yat-sen led the Kuomintang party to victory and ostensible unification.

In the meantime, socialist and communist ideas began to proliferate. The Chinese Communists see the May 4, 1919, movement as the point at which the old revolution ended and the new one began. In 1921 a few Chinese intellectuals organized the Communist party of China and began their spectacular march to power. In 1949 this revolution culminated with the unification of all of China with the exception of Taiwan, the large island off the Chinese coast.

The Chinese Communists have thus received a double heritage: first, the ancient and humane culture of China; and second, the ideology of world communism. The combination of these two aspects, along with its profound nationalism, doubtless accounts for China's achievements since 1949. It should also help in the understanding of China's problems.

Their Achievements. It is idle to underestimate what the Chinese Communists have been able to accomplish. They have unified the country as it has never been before, and they have raised the overall standard of living. They have set into operation a centralized government that has shaped an undisciplined people into a gigantic tool of a dedicated party and in the process generated true nationalism.

Whatever the statistics, China has increased its agricultural production and has taken giant strides in industrialization.

Their Problems. The recognition of their achievements should be matched with an understanding of their problems. How can they maintain the momentum of their growth with the reality of the size and nature of their population? With the margin of subsistence already so slim, how can enough food be provided for so many additional stomachs each year?

China is faced with the enormous cost of its crash program in industrialization, as well as the cost of its administration and military. It also faces the cost and the national effort required to maintain its dominance in Asia and its influence throughout the world.

Reorganized Slash Recall

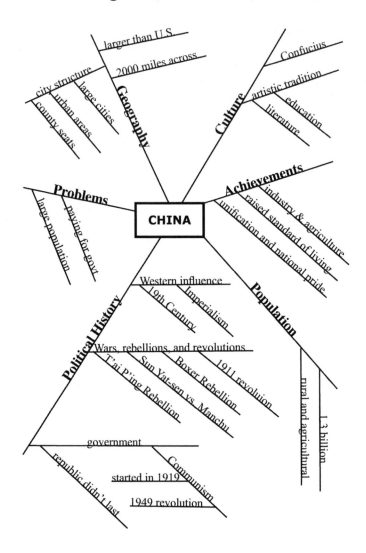

Quiz on China

Test yourself: After studying the lesson on China, apply the study method. Take this quiz to determine how much you learned. Answers are located within the text. Answer the quiz based on what is in the text, not from other sources or personal opinion.

1. Compare China and the United States in terms of "The Land" and "The People."

   _____

   _____

   _____

   _____

2. Describe one important aspect of the Chinese cultural heritage.

   _____

3. List two items or incidents of Western influence on modern China.

   _____

   _____

4. Name two major achievements of the Chinese government.

   _____

   _____

5. Name one major problem that modern China faces.

   _____

Supplemental Practice

Use your hand as a pacer for your daily reading. Compete the following supplemental practice before beginning Lesson Ten:

- Read at least one hour before Lesson Ten, using your hand as a pacer. This reading may be done in any book or magazine of your choice.

- Practice the Study and Depth Reading Drill below at least four times before going on to the next lesson.

- Optional: Practice the Push-Down Drill four times before going on to Lesson Ten.

Study and Depth Reading Drill

If you are not a student, do not feel compelled to study a textbook. Select any informational book on a subject that interests you.

1. Select a chapter or section (it may be very short) in a textbook or a book of nonfiction that represents the most difficult reading you do. (Avoid math or science books that are mainly formulas and problems.)

2. Determine your reading purpose: to know it very thoroughly in order to pass a detailed test; to know it fairly well (to back up main ideas or theories with supporting facts); to become familiar with the main ideas; or to know the thesis of the chapter or section.

3. With your purpose decided, apply the study techniques. Adapt the techniques to meet your purpose.

Use the table on the next page to track your progress.

Practice Report Register

This is a weekly report of your progress at daily practice drills. Ideally, you should see an improvement in rate from day to day and week to week. Make it your goal to attempt ever increasing rates.

First Time	Time spent on drill: _____ mins.	Range of reading rates: ____ to ____ low high	Comments
Second Time	Time spent on drill: _____ mins.	Range of reading rates: ____ to ____ low high	Comments
Third Time	Time spent on drill: _____ mins.	Range of reading rates: ____ to ____ low high	Comments
Fourth Time	Time spent on drill: _____ mins.	Range of reading rates: ____ to ____ low high	Comments

Practice Summary
Record on your Progress Report Chart.

Total Time Spent on Drills: _____

Highest Reading Rate: _____

<u>**What You Need for This Lesson:**</u>

Evelyn Wood Course Guide

Audio CD #5

Pencil or pen

A book and a magazine of your choice

Optional: An electronic document, at least 4 pages long

Evelyn Wood
READING DYNAMICS®
Lesson 10

Breeze Through E-Mail, Letters, and Magazines

Supplemental Practice

Use your hand as a pacer for all your daily reading. Practice the following assignments before going on to Lesson Eleven:

- Read at least one hour before Lesson Eleven, using your hand as a pacer. This reading may be done in any book of your choice.

- Practice the Magazine Reading Drill given below at least four times before going on to the next lesson.

- Optional: Practice the Add Half a Page Drill (track number) four times before going on to the next lesson.

Magazine Reading Drill

1. Select a magazine to read, and overview the table of contents. Check with a pencil the articles that you most want to read, and assign priorities in their order of importance to you. (If there is no table of contents or if it does not give enough information, then quickly—in five minutes—thumb through the magazine, deciding what you want to read and assigning the priorities as you go.)

2. In 15 minutes, cover the whole magazine, reading one or two articles of the highest priority and previewing all others that you feel are important. See how much you can cover each day; you should be able to cover more and more material each time you do this drill. Estimate and record the amount of material covered in 15 minutes.

Use the table on the next page to track your progress.

Practice Report Register

This is a weekly report of your progress at daily practice drills. Ideally, you should see an improvement in rate from day to day and week to week. Make it your goal to attempt ever increasing rates.

First Time	Time spent on drill: _____ mins.	Range of reading rates: ____ to ____ low high	Comments
Second Time	Time spent on drill: _____ mins.	Range of reading rates: ____ to ____ low high	Comments
Third Time	Time spent on drill: _____ mins.	Range of reading rates: ____ to ____ low high	Comments
Fourth Time	Time spent on drill: _____ mins.	Range of reading rates: ____ to ____ low high	Comments

Practice Summary
Record on your Progress Report Chart.

Total Time Spent on Drills: _____

Highest Reading Rate: _____

What You Need for This Lesson:

Evelyn Wood Course Guide

Audio CD #6

Pencil or pen

Blank paper

A book of your choice

Evelyn Wood
READING DYNAMICS®

Lesson 11

Achieve Flexibility in Reading

Reading Techniques to Be Used

1. Linear Read   2. Skim   3. Scan   4. Study Method

866-5931 Wright Richard 102EastAv
838-7641 Wright William J 15CheleneRd
838-6135 Wrigley Mildred E SLedgeRdRwytn
866-7994 Wrinn J J rl est 1 SGlenwoodAvSN
866-1322 Wu George 1-Oakfi eldRdSN
866-6080 -Boys Telephone
866-7881 WuhrerAnde 7-SeasidePlEN
866-1311 WuhrerSam 7-SeasidePlEN
847-9458 Wultf Frank R 195WRocksRd
846-2143 Wuskie Susan 32EastAv
847-0082 Wyman Lewis C 31 Noah'sLa
847-7770 Wynkoop John R Jr 134PerryAv
866-8337 Wynn Edward 29BurrittAvSN

X
——— XEROX CORPORATION———
STMFRD -Sales
329-881 1011HighRidgeRdStamford
853-1333 Fairfi eld County Technical
Service 445HamiltonAv
853-8001 XEXEX INDUSTRIES INC.
SDukePlSN

Y
866-4425 Y M C A 370WestAv
853-2555 Yacht Queen Ann II BeachRdEN
853-4838 Yacht Rita-JCalfPastureBeachRdE
866-6400 Yacht Yankee Girl MackSN
838-0935 Yackulics John J CloverlyCircleEN
866-9003 Yackuiics Mary Mrs 7LocustEN
838-2485 Yager Bertha Mrs
846-1932 Yates Paul 164ERocksRd
853-6860 Yates Walter E 20NTaylorAvSN
838-7405 Yavne Israel Rabbi King
846-3130 Yavne Israel Rabbi 41WolfpitAv
847-9356 Yearout Floyd SilvermineAv
838-2476 Yerinides Gus 29-SummittAvSn
866-9124 Yerinides Joseph 1 SBayviewAvSN 846-
1329 YerkesACraig SAndersenRD
847-3393 Yff Robert SWildwoodLa
838-5005 Yobbagy Arthur 6LincolnAvSoN
838-2288 Yobbagy William 31PhillipsSoN
853-6627 Yoel M H 1 RollingLa
847-0894 Yoppe William J 199PonusAv
838-7802 Yordon Henry K Rev 9William
847-8487 York Glenn P 38-SilvermineAv
847-1603 Yorzinski Alexander 9Girard
853-0837 Yost Charles 11 Elm

846-1744 Yost Edmund W Jr 55NewtownAv
847-4853 Yost Elwood 20GlenAv
847-0265 Yost Harry CamelotDr
838-3235 Youhas Anthony Colony
846-9682 Young Brian 41WolfpitAv
846-1456 YOUNG DECORATORS 554MainAv
846-1594 Young Donald M 24DouglasDr
866-3924 Young Grace J Mrs 14ElmcrestTer
838-5874 Young Harry M 2HawkinsAvEN
866-8752 Young Ivory Sr MontereyPlSN
846-0198 Yuan Kien 21DonohueDr
866-9823 Yunckes Gustav 1-OrlandoRd
866-6956 Yuscak Hazel 22FourthEN

Z
866-1612 Zabelle Realty rl est 104EastAv
836-0050 Zabelle Sidney 6RebellLa
866-6689 Zabelle Travel Agency 104EastAv
846-0200 Zabelle William 45Maple
866-0023 Zacarola John J 9EagleRd
838-8024 Zacc Bill 11 BluffAvRwtyn
854-9614 Zach Philip 40 5 Av
866-4939 Zack William J 14AlrowoodDr
847-4426 Zahlman Gaylord 31 DryHlRd
847-4794 Zahlman Velma Mrs 17BrtittMnr
838-8227 Zaino James V 48BaxterDrSn
838-6352 Zaino John 42-summittAvSN
847-3494 Zaino Patsy SBurlingtonCt
846-9274 Zakar Isidore 48Aiken
866-7112 ZakharAntone 22VanZantEN
866-7753 Zakhar George J 6RolandAvEN
838-9117 Zakhar James 48FifthEN
838-8228 Zakhar Joseph 76GrandviewAv
846-1258 Zakhar Robert SThames
846-9292 Zakhar William J 14HideawayLa
846-1065 Zaleski Frank 26-SurreyDr
847-8606 Zaleski Julius E Sr 20EllS
866-4977 Zambrana Maria 55BoutonSN
838-4361 Zamm Edward J atty 222Main
847-9092 -Res AppletreeLa
838-4066 Zamm Pauline 26MonroeSn
847-2211 Zander Arthur H 21LancasterDr
866-5503 Zanesky Robert atty 110Wall WESTPT
847-8625 Zangrillo Robert InwoodRd
846-9601 ZannellaC 456NewtownAv
846-1702 Zannella Joseph 456NewtownAv

Time Used to Meet Purpose: _____

Reading Techniques to Be Used

1. Linear Read   2. Skim   3. Scan   4. Study Method

Internal Affairs

During the first four years under the constitution, 1954-1958, internal affairs were given priority. The Communists felt obliged to perfect their collective leadership, keep the armed forces at top strength, wrestle with minority problems, do something about Taiwan, maintain "purity" in the party and tighten the processes of thought control. The economic crises came after 1958.

Collective Leadership. Nowhere in the world during those years was there a more impressive leadership than in China. The party and the government worked at every level through interlocking directorates. In towns and villages, the people voted for representatives in local congresses and councils, who received orders telling them what to do from the general secretariat in Beijing. At the national level, the party hierarchy dominated the government and on occasion used an advisory body called the Supreme State Conference as a forum for important pronouncements. It converted the National Defense Council into a mere front for military direction.

Time Used to Meet Purpose: _____

Supplemental Practice

Use your hand as a pacer for all your daily reading. Complete the following assignments before going on to Lesson Twelve:

- Read at least one hour before completing Lesson Twelve, using your hand as a pacer. This reading may be done in any book or magazine of your choice, and it need not be done all at one sitting.

- Practice the Overlap Drill on the next page at least four times before going on to the next lesson.

- Optional: Before beginning Lesson Twelve, review and practice each of the drills from the following lessons: Lessons Three, Four, Five and Seven.

Supplemental Practice

Overlap Drill

1. From any starting point, read for good comprehension as fast as you can for one minute. Write the number "1" where you stop reading.

2. Read on in the new material for another minute. Write the number "2" where you stop reading. Optional: Create a Recall Pattern with information from Sections 1 and 2.

3. Practice read both Sections 1 and 2 in one minute, and be sure to make the mark.

4. Read on from the number "2" mark as fast as you can for one minute. Write the number "3" where you stop.

5. Practice read Sections 1, 2 and 3 in one minute, and make your mark.

6. Read on from the number "3" as fast as you can for comprehension. Write the number "4" where you stop reading. Optional: Add to your Recall Pattern any new information obtained from any parts of the drill.

7. Go back to the number "2" as a starting point, and practice read through Section 4 in one minute.

8. Read on from number "4" as fast as you can for comprehension. Write the number "5" where you stop.

9. Go back to the number "3" as a starting point, and practice read through Section 5 in one minute.

10. Go back to the very beginning as a starting point, and practice read through Section 3 in one minute.

11. Go back to the beginning again, and this time practice read through Section 4, making your mark in one minute.

12. Go back to the beginning again, and practice read through all the sections in one minute. Make your mark!

13. Read in new material for good comprehension as fast as you can for one minute. Compute and record your rate, and add to your recall.

Practice Report Register

This is a weekly report of your progress at daily practice drills. Ideally, you should see an improvement in rate from day to day and week to week. Make it your goal to attempt ever increasing rates.

First Time	Time spent on drill: _____ mins.	Range of reading rates: ____ to ____ low high	Comments
Second Time	Time spent on drill: _____ mins.	Range of reading rates: ____ to ____ low high	Comments
Third Time	Time spent on drill: _____ mins.	Range of reading rates: ____ to ____ low high	Comments
Fourth Time	Time spent on drill: _____ mins.	Range of reading rates: ____ to ____ low high	Comments

Practice Summary
Record on your Progress Report Chart.

Total Time Spent on Drills: _____

Highest Reading Rate: _____

<u>**What You Need for This Lesson:**</u>

Evelyn Wood Course Guide

Audio CD #6

Pencil or pen

Blank paper

A book of your choice

Lesson 12

Evaluate Your Progress

Albert Einstein
by Arthur Beckhard

Chapter Two: Shadows of Prejudices

Uncle Jacob's little game made a vast difference in Albert's work at school. As a matter of fact, it was responsible for much of his later success, for chasing the elusive "X" proved to have so great a fascination for him that mathematics soon became his favorite study. During the following year his marks improved amazingly, and he shot to the head of the class in algebra, geometry and physics.   *70*

Albert did not forget his promise to his parents. He never complained. But the hours spent in the classrooms of the Gymnasium seemed endless and, like the donkey whose master dangled a tempting morsel of new-mown hay just out of reach of his nose, Albert kept himself going from one class to the next by thinking of the fun that awaited him at home—books, talks, and his violin.   *140*

The wonderful evenings at the Einsteins' continued though a rival electrochemical shop was opened just across the street from the Einstein shop, just as Albert's father had foreseen. Business began to taper off. Some of their oldest customers admitted that they were afraid not to take their trade to the new store. They have been told it was owned by someone very high in political and army circles whose influence could be of benefit to them in many ways.   *219*

Hermann and Jacob Einstein had done so well for so long that they had been able to set aside quite a sum of money. At first they were not too concerned by the falling off of their profits. But as time passed and more and more of their customers deserted them, the partners knew something would have to be done before their savings disappeared. They began writing to friends and relatives in other cities and countries, asking if any of them knew of business opportunities.   *139*

Albert knew nothing of this, because his parents and Uncle Jacob were determined that their worries should not cast gloom over their cheerful evenings at home. So it came as a surprise when his parents told him that they were moving to Milan in Italy, where relatives had written to say there was a dry-goods and hardware store available. *364*

It was even a greater shock to the boy when his parents told him that he could not go with them.

"You must finish your schooling so that you can get work, Albert," his father said. "I don't like to have the family separated and I don't like to think of you alone here in Munich, but there is no other way. You can stay at the Weills'. Their boy has gone into the army and they have a room. It will not be like staying with strangers." *452*

"It will be for only a few months at a time," his mother added. "Your father will make enough money so that you will be able to spend the summer vacation with us."

"Of course," Albert said, smiling so that his mother would not cry. "I'll get along fine. It'll be fun being on my own." *508*

He had promised that he would not complain about school and he meant to keep his word. But nobody was fooled. It was a sad day for all of them when Albert and Mr. and Mrs. Weill saw his family off on the little train that was to take them on the first lap of their journey. *565*

Determined to concentrate on his schoolwork so that he could finish the course as quickly as possible, Albert neglected his violin. With every possible minute spent on study, the days passed more quickly than he had dared hope. He had no time for loneliness or self-pity. He did not go to Milan during the summer vacation. Instead, he studied at home in order to get ahead of his class in the hope of being able to skip a year. *645*

There were bad days for Albert. His many questions angered his teachers because they seemed to show that he knew more than they did. He couldn't be punished for this but they were always on the lookout for ways of making him look silly in front of his classmates. Even this was not easy since, with his parents away and no friends or sports to distract him, there was nothing for him to do but study. 712

Perhaps that was why the teachers looked the other way and pretended not to hear when Albert's fellow students began making fun of him for being a Jew. 748

He had always known that his parents were Jewish, and that therefore he probably was too. But he had never thought about it very much or realized that it made him different from his fellow students. 784

His family, while deeply religious, were not followers of the Orthodox faith. They did not believe in the vengeful God of the Old Testament, but in the freedom and dignity of the individual and in the right of every man, woman, and child to worship God in whatever way he chooses. 835

He wished his parents were here so that he could ask them why the other boys and girls looked at him with such anger and bitterness. He wished he could ask them just what it meant to be a Jew. He couldn't ask the Weills. He could not think of an answer. This was not a case where he could call the unknown quantity "X" and seek its meaning in a formula. 906

He had promised his parents he would not complain, but this was different. He could feel the dislike of his classmates. They looked at him as if he had committed a crime. He would have to think of a way to get out of the Gymnasium and still have a chance of getting a diploma. He would keep his promise. He would not complain. And he would think of some means to be of help to his family; but he knew he would not continue in that school. 994

It was a dreary, depressing day. The rain, part sleet, slanted down on the windows of the train. There were five other passengers crowded into the stuffy compartment. There was every reason in the world why Albert should have been depressed, but he was not. To him the train might just as easily have been a golden chariot carrying him to the Royal Ball — or straight up into the clouds, for that matter. He was leaving Germany. Soon he would see his father and mother and Maja! He was going to Milan! 1086

For the hundredth time he looked around anxiously to make sure he still had his belongings. His lunch and supper? Yes — there on the floor under his feet. His clothes? That bulgy brown-paper parcel crowded into the luggage rack overhead. His books? He hoped he'd have no trouble getting the round-topped leather trunk from the baggage compartment in the car's vestibule. He clutched his violin in its wooden case and leaned his head back against the seat. He was actually on his way to Milan! *1172*

As if he were reading about it in a book, he thought how this had been accomplished. It had been much simpler than he imagined once he had made up his mind to leave the school.

He had gone to the school physician and complained that he felt as if he were about to have violent fits. He would often dream of choking his ancient-history professor. As he had expected, the doctor reported the interview to the principal, and Albert had been summoned to the principal's office. *1261*

He had been asked to wait in the anteroom. He had watched his teachers file in one after another to discuss his case with the principal. On the way out they had looked in his direction, some with pity, some in anger, but everyone with an expression of relief. When the principal had called him, his long face had been even more solemn than usual. He had told Albert that it had been decided to give him a certificate of ill-health; that in no way reflected on his standing as a student but that it meant he would be dismissed from the school. He was free to go to any other school or even to return here if he could pass the physical examination. He was free! *1389*

He had hardly been able to keep from shouting it to the people on the streets. He had rushed to the Weills' house and written his father at once asking for the fare to Milan. He had said he was feeling fine, so that they would not worry. *1437*

Mr. Einstein had sent the money and here he was! He was going to see his mother and father, and he felt no sense of guilt. He knew that no one would have taken his "symptoms" seriously unless they'd been as eager to get rid of him as he had been to leave, and they had jumped at the first possible excuse offered. He grinned to himself in the crowded railway carriage. *1509*

His family was overjoyed to see him. His mother exclaimed over and over again that he'd grown so tall she would not have recognized him. Maja too had grown and seemed surprisingly attractive to her big brother. His father and Uncle Jacob regarded him with undisguised pride. As a matter of fact, though he was unaware of it and would not have been interested in any case, he had grown into a very handsome boy with large dark eyes, brown wavy hair and look of great strength.   *1597*

One day he asked them why his fellow students had scorned him for being a Jew.

"We've often talked it over — your mother and Uncle Jacob and I," his father said.   *1628*

"We've wondered whether we should warn you about the way so many people feel about Jews."

"You see, Albert," his mother said, "people really don't know why they feel that way. Some hold our religion against us. Others dislike us as a race."   *1671*

"We didn't tell you the whole truth in Munich, Albert," his father continued. "It was true that the army officers created competition to our store, but it was also true that our customers were told not to buy from us because we were Jews. That's why we came to Milan, where there is no prejudice against our people."   *1729*

"It may be a good thing that this has happened when you are young, Albert," Uncle Jacob added. "It should teach you never to put labels on people because of their race, or the color of their skins. There are good people and bad people in every race. You must learn to judge each person for himself alone."   *1787*

"In other words," Mrs. Einstein finished, "try to be a fine man no matter what race you happen to belong to. We don't think of Mendelssohn as a great Jew. We think of him as a great composer. By the way, how do you intend to be great? Have you any plans?"   *1839*

"Yes," Albert answered unhesitating. "I want to be a teacher."

"No more ideas of earning your living by playing the violin?" His father asked.

"I want to prove that you can help people learn without punishing them," Albert said earnestly. "I want to try to get into Polytechnic Institute in Zurich, Switzerland."

1892

"But that's run by the Swiss Government and admits only Swiss citizens," his mother said.

"Then I will become one. I don't want to be a German anymore. I don't believe it's right for a country to be run by soldiers and by force."

"Albert, you aren't old enough to be a citizen of any place," his mother spoke in laughter.

1955

"Then I'll wait," Albert answered. "Or perhaps when they see how much I know about mathematics they will make some special arrangement for me to get into Polytechnic. Anyway, I'm going to try."

1989

The last thing his parents wished was to shake Albert's self-confidence. They remembered only too well how shy he had been as a child, and they were glad to see that he was now ready to fight for what he believed in. So Mr. Einstein filled out the application for Albert to be allowed to take the entrance examinations to the great Polytechnic Institute which offered junior college courses, college courses and postgraduate work. To his surprise, his school record at the Munich Gymnasium won Albert the chance to take the exams.

2081

Proudly, the family dipped into their savings to send their boy to Switzerland where he took all the necessary examinations. A week later the self-confident young man learned that he had flunked in biology, zoology and all languages.

2121

Chapter Three: Preparatory School

Unlike his teachers at Munich Gymnasium, the professors at the Swiss Federal Polytechnic Institute in Zurich recognized in Albert the making of a great mathematician or physicist. Instead of discouraging him from further attempts to enter the great university, they suggested that he go to a preparatory school in Aarau, Switzerland, for at least a year. There he would be able to make up his deficiencies. Their belief in him gave him new courage. His failure to pass the entrance examinations seemed to him a challenge rather than a defeat. He sent in his application to the school at Aarau without even waiting to write home for advice, and to his great satisfaction, his application was accepted.   *2240*

He did not look forward to his term at Aarau with any pleasure, however. He fully expected to have to drill the dull rules of grammar into his head by endless repetition and grim determination. But he wrote home, packed his few belongings, and set out for the little village that backed up against the great Swiss Alps.   *2298*

To his amazement, nothing was as he had expected it to be. On the contrary the Aarau school gave Albert his first glimpse into what teaching could be like. He found complete freedom here. Students were enrolled at Aarau because they wanted to learn. The faculty was there to help those who needed it. The professors were not martinets. There was no feeling of military discipline. If someone wished to cut a class he cut it. No teacher rebuked him. But if he had difficulty in making up the lost classwork, no one sympathized with him; nor were the other, more conscientious students asked to suffer because of his absence. No lectures were repeated or reviewed. One attended class or had to make up the loss on one's own time.   *2428*

There was a much closer relationship between teacher and pupil than Albert had dreamed could exist. He was amazed to find that he was welcome as a guest in many faculty homes. It was in this way that he came to know and love the delightful Winteller family.   *2456*

Whenever Albert went to visit them, he was reminded vividly of those beloved evenings at home in Munich. The Winteller family loved music as much as the Einsteins did. When Karl and Hans and Maria and the professor and Mrs. Winteller learned that Albert played the violin, he was urged to bring it to their house. Thereafter, they spent many evenings playing chamber music or singing ballads and Lieder, and Albert forgot his homesickness and had a wonderful time.   *2555*

His friendship with the Winteller family had many results. Mrs. Winteller saw to it, as his mother would have had she been there, that the tall, thin, growing boy got enough to eat. Karl, a boy of his own age, became his first friend. Professor Winteller himself was so convinced that Albert had a great deal to offer the world of science and would make an excellent teacher that he wrote about him not only to Mrs. Einstein but to his own friends. It was as a result of these letters that he discovered that an acquaintance of his was a prosperous and distant relative of the Einsteins. This gentleman began sending a little money each month to help Albert pay for his living expenses.   *2680*

Unknown to the kind professor, Albert, instead of using this money to pay for food, clothing and laundry, began to do without socks or hats or overcoats and put aside as much as possible of this money toward the day when he would be old enough to become a Swiss citizen. He had learned that there was a registration fee that must accompany the application for citizenship, and he wanted to be sure that he would have enough money when the time came.   *2764*

It seemed to Albert that he had barely settle down when the year was over. It was difficult to say good-by to the Wintellers who had become such close friends. In all likelihood he would not see any of them soon again, for if he could pass his examinations in the fall, he would be living in Zurich, at a considerable distance from Aarau. Only a week before this unhappy parting, Albert had an inspiration.   *2840*

"Karl, why don't you come to Milan with me for the summer?" he exclaimed.

"That'd be great, Albert, but — perhaps I'd better let you try to persuade Father." Albert was a convincing speaker, and professor Winteller gave his consent to the plan.   *2882*

In Milan, Albert was shocked to discover how thin and ill-looking his father had become. No one had written that Mr. Einstein's health had begun to fail, and that he could spend very little time in the shop. Nevertheless, in spite of their worries, the Einsteins all cheered upon the arrival of the two boys. It soon became apparent, even to Albert who was not very observant of such matters, that Karl was much taken with his little sister, Maja. For a time the three young people went everywhere together. They went to museums and for walks around the beautiful city. They even managed, by waiting in line, to get standing room at the opera for a few lire.   *3001*

It was a wonderful summer for Albert. He had never before had companions of his own age who liked the same things he liked. It was with real regret that he gradually came to realize that his sister and his friend did not always want him with them. When it finally dawned on him that they were in love, the summer was almost over.   *3065*

One morning Karl went in to see Mr. Einstein alone. He told him he wanted to stay on in Milan and go into the Einstein business or at least help out at the store.   *3099*

"It isn't only that I've fallen in love with your daughter, Mr. Einstein," he explained. "I have, and I do want to stay here in Milan to be near her. But I know we're both too young to be married for some time, and that I must make money before I even ask her to become engaged."

"You seem to have thought of everything." Mr. Einstein said, stroking his mustache so as to hide a smile.   *3175*

"There is something else. It's about Albert," Karl said.

"He's worried about the money it will cost for him to go to the Swiss Federal Polytechnic. He sees that the business needs more help. He knows that you are not too well. He doesn't want to create hardships for all of you by leaving and..."

"Did he tell you this?"   *3235*

"No, Mr. Einstein. Albert is going to be a great man some day. My father thinks so. The dean at Aarau thought so."

"I think I know what you mean, Karl," Mr. Einstein said gravely. "I shall always remember something that happened when Albert was about five. He was just getting over the measles, and I used to bring him things to divert him. One day I happened to bring him a small compass. Nothing I had ever brought made so big a hit with him. He couldn't get enough of it. For months after he had recovered he carried it with him, asking questions of anyone who'd listen. What made the arrow move? What force was it that made it turn toward the north? What was magnetism? What was gravity? It was, as you just said, as if he was trying to understand the whole universe — at five." *3384*

"You know, then, how important it is that he go to the Swiss Federal Polytechnic Institute — one of the greatest of its sort in the world?" *3410*

Mr. Einstein nodded. "I'll be proud to accept your offer to take his place here, Karl. It will be fine to have you with us. And I'm sure Maja will be delighted." Mr. Einstein smiled warmly on his prospective son-in-law. *3452*

Albert knew nothing of this. He only knew that the whole family escorted him to see him off when the time came for him to leave for Zurich, and that they all disguised the sorrow of parting by expressing the highest hopes for his success. They knew he would succeed. *3502*

**IF YOU FINISH EARLY,
FOLLOW THE DIRECTIONS ON THE NEXT PAGE.**

If you finish early...

If you finish reading the passage before the tone sounds, IMMEDIATELY BEGIN TIMING the amount of time left until the tone sounds. To compute your reading rate:

- Round off the amount of time you did not use to the nearest quarter minute. For example, 11 seconds would be 1/4 minute.

- Subtract the amount of time you did not use from three minutes to find the amount of time you did use.

- Divide the total number of words (3,502) by the amount of time you used.

Albert Einstein Quiz

Chapter Two: Shadows of Prejudice and Chapter Three: Preparatory School

1. Uncle Jacob's game of chasing the elusive "X": (70 words)
   a. improved Albert's marks amazingly.
   b. provided just a brief fascination for Albert.
   c. became so fascinating for Albert that his grades suffered.
   d. seemed childish to Albert.

2. Albert's family moved to Milan: (364 words)
   a. to find a better climate.
   b. so Mrs. Einstein could be near relatives.
   c. because of falling profits due to pressure from the army.
   d. so they could afford to send Albert to a better school.

3. After Albert's family left for Milan, he stayed: (580 words)
   a. with the Weills', friends of the Einsteins.
   b. at the boarding school.
   c. with his uncle.
   d. with his father's parents.

4. Albert concentrated on his schoolwork: (712 words)
   a. to further demonstrate his abilities to his teachers.
   b. so he could finish the course as quickly as possible and perhaps skip a year.
   c. to rapidly learn more about his favorite subjects.
   d. to spite his teachers.

5. Albert was dismissed from school: (1,437)
   a. with a certificate of ill-health.
   b. because of poor grades.
   c. due to his constant complaining.
   d. because his parents ran out of money.

6. After Albert arrived in Milan, his parents noticed: (1,630)
   a. that he had grown thin.
   b. that he talked a great deal about his studies.
   c. that he looked worried despite his excitement.
   d. that he had grown tall, handsome, and strong.

7. Albert told his parents he wanted to be a chemist. (1,900)
   True   False

8. When Albert attended preparatory school in Switzerland: (2,480)
   a. he found hints of the same military discipline he had encountered in Germany.
   b. he was amazed to find school enjoyable.
   c. he began to realize why his classmates didn't like him.
   d. he was still unable to get close to his teachers.

9. What was the name of Albert's new friend who went home to Milan with him for the summer? (2,882)
   a. Maria
   b. Karl
   c. Hans
   d. Marcel

10. Mr. Einstein's health began to fail to the point where he could spend very little time in the shop. (2,960)
    True   False

Calculating Comprehension Scores

Number of Questions Responsible for Answering

		1	2	3	4	5	6	7	8	9	10
Number of Answers Correct	1	100	50	33	25	20	16	14	13	11	10
	2		100	67	50	40	33	29	25	22	20
	3			100	75	60	50	43	38	33	30
	4				100	80	67	57	50	44	40
	5					100	83	72	63	56	50
	6						100	86	75	67	60
	7							100	88	78	70
	8								100	89	80
	9									100	90
	10										100

Recall Sheet

Write everything you remember from the selection you have read. Do NOT look back at the reading. Write only one item on each line.

More Important Points	Details & Supporting Points

Go on to the next page if you need more room.

Recall Sheet (continued)

More Important Points	Details & Supporting Points

Total number of Important Points:_____

Total number of Supporting Points: _____

Could you have written more with more time: _____

Average words per minute reading rate: _____

Evelyn Wood
READING DYNAMICS®
Appendix

Teaching Evelyn Wood Reading Dynamics to Children

Adult graduates of the Evelyn Wood Reading Dynamics program often have a common reaction: "I wish I had known this earlier!" If you have the opportunity to share this with the children in your life -- take it!! Decide how best to share the program based on the child's age, reading ability, and interest in learning the concepts. Here are a few suggestions:

- Work with children who already know how to read, even if it is just at a fundamental level.

- Involve the children's teachers in what you are doing. This program teaches some non-traditional techniques, and having the teacher's support while the child is using these techniques at school will be very helpful.

- For children in elementary and middle school, find age appropriate reading materials to replace the reading materials in this Course Book. Older students can use what is in the Course Book, or any material they enjoy reading.

- If they seem resistant to wanting to learn this program, get them seeing results right away!! Rather than take them through the whole program, guide them through a few critical points to generate interest:

    - Have them take the pre-test. (Lesson 1)

    - Walk them through the Beach Ball Exercise. (Lesson 1)

    - Show them how to use the Underlining Hand Movement. (Lesson 2)

    - Have them listen to and compete the Upside-Down

    - Drill and the reading that follows. (Lesson 2).

    - Most students notice improvement in their rate at this point. This should increase their interest in the rest of the program.

- Use the child's age and interest level to decide how much of the theory behind the techniques to share. Older, interested students can go through the program completely, while you might want to take younger students through the drills.

Answers to Quizzes

Lesson 1: Preassessment *Chasing the "X"*

1. C
2. False
3. B
4. Ulm
5. C
6. D
7. True
8. A
9. Munich
10. D

Lesson 3: *"Take Over Bos'n"*

1. Gun, pistol, Luger
2. 20 or 21
3. Barrett or Jeff Barrett
4. 72 hours
5. The Atlantic Ocean, east of Ascension.
6. Hot, scorching
7. 9
8. The water or the canteen.
9. Bloodshot eyes, cheeks sunken, bearded, ragged, halfnaked
10. He took over and protected the water.

Lesson 12: Post-Assessment *Albert Einstein*

1. A
2. C
3. A
4. B
5. A
6. D
7. False
8. B
9. B
10. True

Summary of Drills

Drill

Lesson One:
Pacing Drill

Lesson Two:
Extension Drill

Lesson Three:
Push-Down Drill*

Lesson Four:
Add Half a Page Drill*
Basic Recall Drill

Lesson Five:
Push-Up Drill*

Lesson Six:
Newspaper Reading Drill

Lesson Seven:
Lazy "S" Hand Movement Drill
Multiple Reading Process Drill

Lesson Eight:
Power Drill*

Lesson Nine:
Study Reading Drill

Lesson Eleven:
Overlap Drill*
Flexibility Drill

Lesson Twelve:
Combination Push-Down/Power/Recall*

This drill is good for reviewing and extra practice.

Progress Report Chart for _____

Lesson One:
Beginning Rate: _____ WPM
Comprehension Score: _____

Number of items recalled:
Major: _____   Minor: _____
Total: _____

Lesson Two:
W-A-T-E-R Rate: _____
Extension Drill Rate: _____
Ending Reading Rate: _____

Supplementary Practice
# of Extension Drills: _____
Highest Reading Rate: _____

Lesson Three:
Opening Reading Rate: _____
Push-Down Drill Rate: _____
Ending Reading Rate: _____

Supplementary Practice
# of Push-Down Drills: _____
Highest Reading Rate: _____

Lesson Four:
Opening Reading Rate: _____
Add Half a Page Drill: _____

Supplementary Practice
# of Add Half a Page Drills: _____
Highest Reading Rate: _____

Lesson Five:
Push-Up Drill Start: _____
Push-Up Drill Finish: _____

Supplementary Practice
# of Push-Up Drills: _____
Highest Reading Rate: _____

Lesson Six:
Ending Reading Rate: _____

Supplementary Practice
# of pages in 10 minutes
Day 1: _____   Day 2: _____
Day 3: _____   Day 4: _____

# of Push-Up Drills: _____
Highest Reading Rate: _____

Progress Report Chart for _____

Lesson Seven:
Opening Reading Rate: _____
Ending Reading Rate: _____

Supplementary Practice
# of Dynamic Drills: _____
Highest Reading Rate: _____

Lesson Eight:
Power Drill Rate: _____

Supplementary Practice
# of Dynamic Drills: _____
Highest Reading Rate: _____

Lesson Nine:
Opening Reading Rate: _____

Supplementary Practice
# of Study/Depth Drills: _____
Highest Reading Rate: _____
# of Push-Down Drills: _____
Highest Reading Rate: _____

Lesson Ten:
Opening Reading Rate: _____
On-Screen 'Old' Rate: _____
On-Screen 'Pace'" Rate: _____

Supplementary Practice
# of pages in 15 minutes
Day 1: _____ Day 2: _____
Day 3: _____ Day 4: _____
# of Add Half a Page Drills:
Highest Reading Rate: ____

Lesson Eleven:
Overlap Drill Rate: _____

Supplementary Practice
# of Overlap Drills: _____
Optional Review of Drills:
3: _____ 4: _____
5: _____ 7: _____

Lesson Twelve:
Opening Reading Rate: _____
Combination Drill Rate: _____
Final Reading Rate: _____

Comprehension Score: _____
Number of items recalled
Major: _____ Minor: _____
Total: _____

Progress Report Chart for _____

Lesson One:
Beginning Rate: _____ WPM
Comprehension Score: _____

Number of items recalled:
Major: _____ Minor: _____
Total: _____

Lesson Two:
W-A-T-E-R Rate: _____
Extension Drill Rate: _____
Ending Reading Rate: _____

Supplementary Practice
# of Extension Drills: _____
Highest Reading Rate: _____

Lesson Three:
Opening Reading Rate: _____
Push-Down Drill Rate: _____
Ending Reading Rate: _____

Supplementary Practice
# of Push-Down Drills: _____
Highest Reading Rate: _____

Lesson Four:
Opening Reading Rate: _____
Add Half a Page Drill: _____

Supplementary Practice
# of Add Half a Page Drills: _____
Highest Reading Rate: _____

Lesson Five:
Push-Up Drill Start: _____
Push-Up Drill Finish: _____

Supplementary Practice
# of Push-Up Drills: _____
Highest Reading Rate: _____

Lesson Six:
Ending Reading Rate: _____

Supplementary Practice
# of pages in 10 minutes
Day 1: _____ Day 2: _____
Day 3: _____ Day 4: _____

# of Push-Up Drills: _____
Highest Reading Rate: _____

Progress Report Chart for _____

Lesson Seven:
Opening Reading Rate: _____
Ending Reading Rate: _____

Supplementary Practice
# of Dynamic Drills: _____
Highest Reading Rate: _____

Lesson Eight:
Power Drill Rate: _____

Supplementary Practice
# of Dynamic Drills: _____
Highest Reading Rate: _____

Lesson Nine:
Opening Reading Rate: _____

Supplementary Practice
# of Study/Depth Drills: _____
Highest Reading Rate: _____
# of Push-Down Drills: _____
Highest Reading Rate: _____

Lesson Ten:
Opening Reading Rate: _____
On-Screen 'Old' Rate: _____
On-Screen 'Pace'" Rate: _____

Supplementary Practice
# of pages in 15 minutes
Day 1: _____ Day 2: _____
Day 3: _____ Day 4: _____
# of Add Half a Page Drills:
Highest Reading Rate: _____

Lesson Eleven:
Overlap Drill Rate: _____

Supplementary Practice
# of Overlap Drills: _____
Optional Review of Drills:
3: _____   4: _____
5: _____   7: _____

Lesson Twelve:
Opening Reading Rate: _____
Combination Drill Rate: _____
Final Reading Rate: _____

Comprehension Score: _____
Number of items recalled
Major: _____   Minor: _____
Total: _____

Happy Reading!

WHEN BEES BUZZ

A Dixie Days Novel

CHRISTY BREEDLOVE

TURNIP PRESS PUBLISHING — MONROE, GEORGIA

When Bees Buzz - A Dixie Days Novel

Copyright © Christy Breedlove 2019

All characters in this book, are fictitious. Any resemblance to actual persons, living or dead, is purely coincidental.

All rights reserved